* * * * * *

"Bringing a deep expertise in ACT to one of the most common and frustrating struggles, this book offers practical tools to move forward and the invaluable gift of greater self-understanding."
—Natasha Daniels, LCSW, author of *Crushing OCD Workbook for Kids*

* * * * * *

"This big-impact book is packed with expert insights and suggestions to help you make sense of your procrastination patterns, stand up to difficult emotions and take confidence-boosting, actionable steps toward greater productivity and a joyful life."
—Joel Minden, Ph.D., author of *Show Your Anxiety Who's Boss*

* * * * * *

"This practical workbook guides the reader past those processes that block action, making you overlook what truly matters. You learn about 'compassionate accountability', 'ruling thoughts' and 'pesky feelings'. The wise 'Tale of Two Arrows' illuminates your relationship with your critical self. I highly recommend it!"
—Dr. Sally Winston, co-author of *Overcoming Anticipatory Anxiety*

* * * * * *

"Whether you're a clinician or a client, this book is extremely useful! We've all procrastinated in our lives, and this book will help you understand what drives you to procrastinate and provide you with evidence-based tools to take more action and make fewer excuses."
—Daniel Granados Salazar, co-chair of the Developing Nations Committee, ACBS

* * * * * *

T0413246

* * * * * *

"Procrastination is the time-honored art of identifying tasks that we find difficult or painful, and then extending our discomfort around those tasks for as long as possible. Like any skill, our ability to put things off develops over a lifetime and can eventually become second nature. Even if you've mastered the art, this book offers a different path. It starts with a clear description of the tricky psychology behind procrastination, and lays bare the myths that maintain it. Then it challenges you to be clearer about your deepest wishes in life and who you want to be. Finally, it guides you through a new practice of Compassionate Accountability that will help you bring your day-to-day choices more fully into alignment with what you really value.

Dr. Zurita Ona's clear, practical guide offers a more direct path between you and the things you want to accomplish. It reveals how even the way we set goals or apparent efforts at 'increasing productivity' can be traps. This is a book about changing your relationship with time and letting go of the exhausting struggle to avoid doing the things that matter. I highly recommend it!"

—Chad LeJeune, Ph.D., founding fellow of the Academy of Cognitive and Behavioral Therapies and author of *The Worry Trap* and *"Pure O" OCD*

* * * * * *

"Twenty years of planning, hoping and avoiding writing a book. I know all the tricks and excuses the anxious mind can come up with. I'm now deep into writing my own. Open this book and get to work."

—Julian McNally, principal psychologist at The Act of Living

* * * * * *

"A compassionate, practical guide for anyone looking to reduce avoidance and live with greater intention. With rich case examples and engaging experiential exercises, this workbook brings Acceptance and Commitment Therapy to life—a must-read for all procrastinators."

—Jill Stoddard, author of *The Big Book of ACT Metaphors*, *Be Mighty* and *Imposter No More*

* * * * * *

The ACT Workbook for the Anxious Procrastinator

The ACT Workbook for the Anxious Procrastinator

How to Accept Yourself, Get Things
Done and Do More of What Matters

PATRICIA E. ZURITA ONA, PSY.D.

Jessica Kingsley Publishers
London and Philadelphia

First published in Great Britain in 2025 by Jessica Kingsley Publishers
An imprint of John Murray Press

1

Copyright © Patricia E. Zurita Ona 2025

The right of Patricia E. Zurita Ona to be identified as the
Author of the Work has been asserted by her in accordance
with the Copyright, Designs and Patents Act 1988.

A CIP catalogue record for this title is available from
the British Library and the Library of Congress

ISBN 978 1 80501 211 5
eISBN 978 1 80501 210 8

Printed and bound in Great Britain by Bell & Bain Limited

Jessica Kingsley Publishers' policy is to use papers that
are natural, renewable and recyclable products and made
from wood grown in sustainable forests. The logging and
manufacturing processes are expected to conform to the
environmental regulations of the country of origin.

Jessica Kingsley Publishers
Carmelite House
50 Victoria Embankment
London EC4Y 0DZ

www.jkp.com

John Murray Press
Part of Hodder & Stoughton Ltd
An Hachette Company

The authorised representative in the EEA is Hachette Ireland,
8 Castlecourt Centre, Dublin 15, D15 XTP3, Ireland (email: info@hbgi.ie)

Contents

Acknowledgments

Writing a book is a unique, challenging, fun, exhilarating and exhausting experience. It's also a time of connection.

Over the years, I have learned that whether I'm struggling, celebrating, or simply navigating the writing process, having people who genuinely support my passions is invaluable.

First, my heartfelt appreciation goes to my clients for their ongoing courage in making bold moves in their lives. Every conversation we've had has been a strong driving force for me to continue creating actionable resources. Thank you for inspiring me!

To my friends—Mateito, Matt, my professor Russ, D.J., Shelly, Jenn (the Hot Mama), Georgi-lu-lu-lu, Ivy and Ben—thank you for sticking with me through my comments, questions, and random texts about procrastination. Your support means a lot to me!

To my colleagues at the East Bay Behavior Therapy Center, thank you tons for your patience! A special thanks to Eunice for gathering over a hundred research articles for me to dive into!

To Jane from JKP and the JKP Team, thank you for showing how much you care about this project!

To my family, thank you for teaching me the importance of pursuing what matters and staying true to my passions.

Finally, my deep gratitude goes to the ACT community!

Start Here

I'll be honest, writing introductions isn't exactly my favorite thing. But what I love is giving you a road map of what to expect and how to make the best of a workbook from the beginning. Here we go!

Over the past 17 years, as a licensed psychologist and coach, working with people of all ages struggling with different types of anxiety, I have seen firsthand the late penalties, frustrations, disappointments, shame, missed deadlines, good intentions, forgotten appointments, or avoidance of difficult conversations of my clients suffering with procrastination.

This workbook is born out of all those countless moments when we—my clients and I—needed to slow down, check what was pushing them to postpone their life, and work together on evidence-based skills to overcome procrastination.

At its core, procrastination is the result of six core psychological processes that have been overly reinforced over time. Procrastination has nothing to do with being lazy or personality traits, or not being action-oriented; it's about "not-knowing" how to effectively manage the psychological drivers beneath it.

You're holding in your hands a full program, based on Acceptance and Commitment Therapy (ACT), that will help you fully understand what leads you to put things off and teach you the fundamental skills you need to get things done and build a life you're proud of.

Chapter by chapter, exercise by exercise, and skill by skill, I'll guide you as if you're climbing a mountain, and I'm right there with you, coaching you and pointing out your next step.

Here are a few clarifications and recommendations for you to make the best of this workbook.

ABOUT THE ORGANIZATION OF THIS WORKBOOK

This workbook is divided into eight chapters, each of which includes specific skills, concepts, experiential exercises, reflective questions, hands-on activities to practice, and a brief summary at the end.

Chapters 1 and 2 lay out the foundation of what procrastination is, what maintains procrastinating habits, the six core psychological drivers behind underlying procrastination, the different misconceptions about procrastination, and the interaction of procrastination with other mental health struggles.

Chapters 3, 4, 5, and 6 teach you skills to tackle those six core psychological processes underlying all procrastinating behaviors.

Chapters 7 and 8 introduce you to core productivity skills to help you stay on task, initiate tasks, manage your time, and organize your schedule and to-do lists.

ABOUT THE EXAMPLES IN THIS WORKBOOK

The examples throughout this workbook are a combination of fictional characters and real-life stories from people I've encountered in both my personal and professional life. All scenarios have been carefully modified and fully de-identified to protect confidentiality.

HOW TO MAKE THE MOST OF THIS WORKBOOK

Here are my reading tips for you!

Work through this workbook from beginning to end

Although it can be tempting, please don't jump chapters, skip exercises, or rush through this book.

This workbook is designed to be read cover to cover, with each chapter building on the previous one. While it might be tempting to jump ahead to sections that seem more relevant to you, I encourage you to trust the flow of this program.

The different pieces of information and skills are interwoven and build on each other; skipping chapters or skills may get you confused, head you in the wrong direction, and minimize the outcomes of using this workbook.

Pace yourself

It's natural you may want results, right now, right away. But procrastinating habits have developed over a long time; in the same way, changing these habits requires practice, patience and time.

I would love for you to work on this workbook at a rhythm that allows you to be fully present with the content of it, gives you time to put skills into action and complete experiential exercises, and furthermore, gives you a firsthand experience of what you're learning.

This workbook is about building awareness of the skills you practice, how you practice them, why you do so, and how they work for you. When needed, it may be beneficial for you to re-read parts of a chapter or practice activities several times to deepen your learning.

Make this workbook yours

This workbook has been written for YOU!

Please highlight, underline, take notes, doodle in the margins, and personalize all pages in any way that helps you to connect with the skills from it.

Treat this workbook as yours by engaging with its content in any possible way that is helpful to you.

This is not a workbook to put on your bookshelf as an ornament to collect dust or to be on the pile of books on your nightstand that are never read. This is a book for you to make the best of your life!

Make a habit to practice your skills

Knowing about a skill is one thing, but regularly practicing it makes all the difference. When you put a skill or principle into action, it gives you first-hand experience with it, so in the future you don't get stuck in your head trying to figure out what to do when having urges to procrastinate a task.

So, I beg you to try all the skills from this program, tweak them, make them yours, and, most importantly, put them into action.

Make room to be uncomfortable

You may find some exercises or activities difficult, and feel unsettled or uncomfortable when trying them.

I have been there too; some of the exercises felt unusual when I was learning ACT and attending workshops. I still feel uncomfortable at times when managing my triggers, but I know it's worth doing so.

Please try all exercises with genuine openness, always checking your internal experience and doing what's doable for you.

Building new habits is not about rushing into things or checking things off from a list; it's about making room for your discomfort and checking what you're open and willing to experience in that moment. If some exercises feel too uncomfortable, you can try them for a shorter time or go back to them later after taking a mini break.

Connect with others

Procrastination makes you hide and feel alone in your struggle, which deprives you of one of the most important tools to get back on top of your life: connecting with others.

When you share how procrastination affects you, you'll find that others can relate to you and share a caring moment. Also, sharing what you're learning and how you're using skills can keep you accountable, destigmatize procrastination, and nourish an authentic connection with others.

WHAT'S NEXT AFTER READING THIS WORKBOOK?

When working on a writing project, I usually end up with extra words, ideas, exercises, and skills. This time, instead of saving the extra material on my laptop, I created an online class, ACT beyond Procrastination, at www.thisisdoctorz.com that is filled with additional resources. Take a look at it when you have a chance!

I've worked hard to provide you with ACT skills to tackle procrastinating habits in a simple, uncomplicated, unpretentious, and jargon-free manner. But more importantly, on every page, I'm sharing with you all the skills and principles I teach my clients to stop procrastinating, be who they want to be, and build a life they're proud of. I hope for the same for you!

Warmly,
Dr. Z.
Patricia E. Zurita Ona, Psy.D.

CHAPTER 1

HOW DID I END UP HERE?

Over the last 18 years, I have collaborated with people who, like you, want to have caring friendships, a solid career, fun hobbies, and an overall joyful life, but who have got stuck in an unhelpful pattern of procrastinating behaviors and a rollercoaster of anxiety. Session by session, skill by skill, and choice by choice, I have seen them making bold changes in their lives toward a rich life.

Chapter by chapter, based on Acceptance and Commitment Therapy, I'll share with you my approach to tackling procrastinating behaviors in an actionable, compassionate, and skillful way, so you can also make the bold moves you need to make.

Which option(s) describes you at the moment?

- I want to understand why I procrastinate.
- I want to stop procrastinating.
- I want to learn how other mental health struggles make me procrastinate, and what to do about it.

You will get answers and skills for each one of those options.

Let's start by clarifying that procrastination is not a personality trait, but a pattern of learned behaviors that have been reinforced over and over in your life. You weren't born with a procrastination gene; it happened that over time, the way that you thought about particular projects, the way you felt about them, and the choices you made in those moments fed into a pattern of procrastination that repeated itself multiple times and hurt you and the ones you care about in the long run.

In this workbook, we'll unpack together what drives those procrastinating actions and the skills you need to get things done and build a new pattern of workable behaviors toward the life you want to live.

THE PSYCHOLOGICAL PROCESSES THAT UNDERLIE PROCRASTINATING BEHAVIORS

To start overcoming procrastination you need to be clear about what holds you back from taking action and keeps you stuck in a procrastinating pattern; within ACT, we call those factors "psychological processes."

There are six psychological processes or drivers that intertwine and are behind all your procrastinating actions:

1. You have a hard time sitting with uncomfortable emotions: *non-acceptance of difficult emotions.*
2. You quickly accept all reasons to procrastinate that show up in your mind as the absolute truth: *going along with reasons.*
3. You hold on to rules about what you need to get things done: *adherence to self-imposed rules.*
4. You doubt yourself and your abilities to get things done: *attachment to self-doubtful thoughts and negative narratives about yourself.*
5. You make impulsive choices focused only on the moment: *proneness to impulsive feeling-based and short-term choices.*
6. You ignore what truly matters to you in the long run: *disconnection from personal values.*

Understanding what's at the core of this pattern of procrastination is key to making a shift in your life. Too often, supposed solutions focus only on the consequences of procrastinating; this is a bit like putting a Band-Aid on a wound.

Effectively addressing procrastinating behaviors requires much more than quick fixes or time-management hacks; it is only by getting to the root of what drives problematic procrastination that you can make real shifts in your life, your relationships and the relationship with yourself.

Let's dive into each one of these psychological processes.

Non-acceptance: You have a difficult time sitting with uncomfortable emotions

In the seminal paper by Feyzi Behnagh and Ferrari (2022), the relationship between different emotional states and procrastinating behaviors were reviewed; the emotions examined in detail were anxiety, fear, shame, guilt, regret, boredom, frustration, anger, and revenge.

Here is the deal: When you feel bored, anxious, or frustrated when initiating a task, you may feel overwhelmed by those feelings, and as a result, you choose to postpone them, distract yourself with other projects, work on a not-so-important task, or choose immediately a more pleasant experience.

Avoiding anything that makes you feel uncomfortable makes perfect sense; everyone does it. I do that too. I avoid watching violent movies or thrillers because I get too scared and then have nightmares.

However, chronically avoiding uncomfortable feelings that come along with a task you need to take care of or a conversation you need to have keeps you stuck in your life.

Some emotional states—fear of failure, anxiety, shame—cause you to procrastinate; you need to get better at feeling and sensing all the emotions that show up the moment you are approaching a task.

Going along with reasons: You quickly accept all reasons to procrastinate that show up in your mind as the absolute truth

Your mind is relentless and creative at presenting you with reasonable and logical thoughts that push you to procrastinate on a task. Here are some examples:

- I won't finish on time, even if I start now…
- This stuff happened to me…
- I need to think about it some more.
- It's not ready, yet.

Those thoughts are called "reason-giving thoughts." I have heard thousands of variations of them; they all sound convincing and make sense in the heat of the moment when facing a particular task. The challenge is that by holding on to them as commands of your actions, you put off stuff that matters to you.

Adherence to self-imposed rules: You hold on to inflexible thoughts about what you need to get things done

There is a particular type of thought that your mind comes up with about "all the stuff you need to feel or have to start working on a project." Here are some examples:

- I need to feel good to do this task: "I'm just not feeling it."
- I work better under stress/last minute.
- I'll do it when I get there.
- I need to have a solid plan before I start…

Of course, it's appropriate that you want or need to have a particular setting to get things done; yet these thoughts are powerful because you are treating them as "unbreakable rules." That's why they're called ruling thoughts, and as a result, you end up procrastinating and getting further away from the life you want to live.

Attachment to self-doubts: You doubt yourself and your ability to take care of things

Different researchers, Steel (2007), Burka and Yuen (1983), Basco (2009), and Sirois (2014), have identified self-doubt, indecision, and self-criticizing thoughts as prominent in procrastinating behaviors.

Here are some examples of self-doubtful thoughts:

- Can I do it?
- What if I make a bad decision?
- Is this the right way of doing it?
- What if I make a wrong choice and things don't work out well?
- If I make a poor choice, people will get cranky with me.

It's natural to doubt ourselves, question our confidence, be hesitant about certain decisions, or be uncertain about the outcome of a project. It's not easy to experience any type of self-doubt; it's quite uncomfortable.

However, as annoying as doubtful thoughts are, they're not the problem; the problem is doing exactly what those thoughts push you to do and feeding quickly into a procrastination pattern.

Proneness to impulsive and short-term choices: You make impulsive choices focused only on the moment

How often in the spirit of the moment have you chosen to do something more pleasant or fun than face the tediousness of the task you need to take care of? When looking at procrastinating behaviors, this is a very common response to the distress that you experience when encountering a task that doesn't seem pleasant, fun, or exciting.

You act rashly and don't see or can't foresee the consequences of your choices in the long run. It's like you're focused on what you need and want in that precise moment; and interestingly, in that moment, those decisions don't feel rash to you. They feel necessary because of the internal discomfort you're experiencing when attempting to take care of things.

Unfortunately, feeling-based and short-term choices add fuel to the cycle of procrastination because nourishing your relationships, fostering a joyful life, and putting your energy into what's important to you require that you instead make values-based choices that impact your life in the long run.

Disconnection from your personal values: You ignore what truly matters to you in the long run

Quite often my clients say things like, "I want to do my job but don't see the point of working on that proposal; I don't see how that report would help my manager in this meeting—it's a waste of time."

At a time in which our to-do lists grow by the minute and many mundane tasks require our attention, I can see you rolling your eyes at all those activities you have been putting off and thinking of them as irrelevant, unimportant, and insignificant.

I'm not saying that every mundane task—cleaning the kitchen or paying your taxes—is equal in meaning. I certainly struggle to find meaning when doing laundry or folding clothes; there is clearly variability in how things matter to each one of us based on our individual values.

But, what I'm saying is that each one of those activities has a cumulative effect on the quality of our lives in the long run. If you're unable to contact your values when looking at the different tasks you need to take care of and ignore the impact of those tasks in your life in the long term, you are more likely to procrastinate and get further away from building a life you're proud of.

WHY THE SIX PSYCHOLOGICAL PROCESSES MATTER

You just finished learning about the roots of procrastination, yay! You may still be wondering, why is this important?

Here is my response—instead of thinking of procrastination as a personality trait, as if something is permanently broken with you or that you're always going to be a lazy person, now you know that those psychological processes are the ones that push you to engage in procrastinating behaviors. Think of these processes as the engine of a car that, instead of driving toward what matters to you, pushes you to drive in the direction of avoidance.

Think for a moment of Abhi, an engineer, working at a biotech company. He's smart, kind, funny, and loves to play soccer. Yet, he has been struggling with procrastination since middle school.

Abhi needs to complete an executive report for this manager; he was assigned this task a month ago. But every time he thinks about starting to work on it, he tells himself, "There is still time, it's too early; I have three weeks to finish it. I'm fast with numbers, I'll be okay," so he starts answering his emails and feels productive emptying his inbox. Another time, Abhi quickly scans the requirements of this executive report, visualizes in his mind the way he will present the data, and as he's imagining the structure of the report, he sighs, and says, "I got this, I'm fine."

"I won't make it, it's too close; the numbers won't make sense; aughhh," thinks Abhi, as he sits in front of his laptop a week before his deadline. He opens the folder with documents he needs to analyze and feels nervousness in his whole body about the deadline. "I have to analyze the dates of 12 more projects; this is a lot, it's hard work; I won't do it right," he thinks, as the tension in his body increases.

"I'm going home; I will order some food and continue working on the report; I'll make it happen," thinks Abhi, as he drives back to his apartment on a sunny summer day.

As he opens the door of his apartment, he notices stiffness in his shoulders, has the intention to advance this report, orders his favorite pizza, pepperoni, and thinks, "I need a break; I worked hard today, and I need to be in the right mood to continue working." He turns on the TV and watches his favorite episode of *Curb Your Enthusiasm* to cheer himself up.

The following day, Abhi attempts to analyze the data of the second project, but as he's starting to do so, he realizes that "he needs to have the right statistical software" for this project. So he frantically starts researching three different types of statistical software, searches for comparison charts, reads reviews of people that have used each one of these programs, and sends emails asking questions about these platforms; by noon, he feels stressed and doesn't know which program he's going buy since they all look similar.

"This is too much; I can't do it. I should have started sooner; I'm doing everything I can, but this project is complex. I need to have the right tools." He's looking at his watch while walking fast to get a cup of coffee.

"Please email me the report." Abhi imagines his boss asking for the report as he sips a cup of lukewarm coffee. He breathes heavily and faster, feels ashamed, and feels like hiding from everyone in the office. Abhi goes back quickly to his desk and fills different slots from the previous weeks on his schedule so it looks as if he has been working on this project for a while. "Hope nobody finds out."

"What's wrong with me? Why didn't I start working on this project earlier? There is something wrong with me. I'm a loser…it's me…it's me." Abhi feels overwhelmed, guilty, and almost nauseated as it is the day before the deadline. He calls his best friend to tell him what's going on.

"I can't stand this; this is unbearable. Why bother? There is no way I'll finish this report on time. It sucks. I suck. Why bother even pretending?"

Abhi calls his office and requests a day off. He collapses on his couch as he turns on the TV to watch the local news. His body is exhausted; he's emotionally exhausted. He's also relieved he doesn't have to see his boss that day.

"I'll never procrastinate again."

Despite Abhi's determination to never procrastinate again, he hasn't delivered projects within the requested deadlines for over a year, and he's still working on some reports that were assigned to him five months ago. He has had many conversations with different managers about his difficulties finishing projects on time. He's close to losing his job.

Procrastinating behaviors work in the short term because every time you procrastinate you're playing-it-safe, so you don't have to experience any uncomfortable experiences in the moment; but the more you play-it-safe by putting things off, the more you struggle with persistent self-doubt, criticism, and shame, leaving you living a life that you don't love. That's how the cycle of procrastination works.

Now that you have a feel for what drives procrastinating behaviors, let's check how these core psychological processes show up in your life.

ACTIVITY: Build a picture of these processes in your life

Think about that moment in time when you couldn't get started on a project or put it off. Next, map and describe each one of these processes that kept you stuck in that procrastinating episode. Do your best to go back in time to what you were thinking, feeling, sensing, and doing in that moment.

• What are the emotions that were very uncomfortable to you?

. . . .

. . . .

. . . .

. . . .

- What are the reasons you go along with when procrastinating?

  . . . .

  . . . .

  . . . .

  . . . .

- What are the rules that you hold on to that led you to procrastinate?

  . . . .

  . . . .

  . . . .

  . . . .

- What are the thoughts about yourself or your ability to get things done that got in your way?

  . . . .

  . . . .

  . . . .

  . . . .

- What are short-term choices you made in that moment?

  . . . .

  . . . .

  . . . .

  . . . .

- What are the areas of your life and things you care about—your values—that got affected in the long run?

. . . .

. . . .

. . . .

. . . .

WRAPPING UP

A procrastinating pattern has nothing to do with a lack of discipline, moral decay, or laziness. It's also not about you being incapable of taking action.

If you don't know how to manage self-criticism, doubts about your competence, catastrophic thoughts, rigid rules, or uncomfortable feelings when approaching tasks, and if you struggle to see the personal relevance of certain tasks, you will naturally do the best you can to ease that emotional strain and protect yourself from it by making quick decisions to avoid what triggers it. Procrastinating behaviors, in this sense, are a form of avoidant behaviors.

All those procrastinating habits often seem effective and work quickly because they allow you to sidestep the internal turmoil of facing your to-do list, as well as external pressure, like worrying about people's disappointment when deadlines are missed. Over time, procrastination has become your comfort zone, the place you retreat to whenever you're confronted with a project, task, activity, or difficult conversation.

You've picked up this workbook because you want to make a shift in your life, conquer procrastination, and focus on what's truly important to you. You, like Abhi, need to learn skills and foster a new mindset that helps you to manage those key psychological processes, get things done, and build a joyful life.

CHAPTER 2

BREAKING THE MYTH OF THE TYPICAL PROCRASTINATOR

Different authors and researchers have described different types of procrastinators: thrill seekers, avoiders, and indecisive (Ferrari and Tyce 2000); avoidant, disorganized, self-doubting, interpersonal, all or nothing, pleasure-seeking (Basco 2009; Pychyl, Morin, and Salmon 2000). I'm sure there are many more categories out there in social media, and who knows many other labels will emerge in the next couple of years.

Procrastinating behaviors look completely different from one person to the other because some people may struggle with some of the processes more than others. Some people who suffer from procrastination are very attuned to the uncomfortable emotions that show up when approaching a task; others are hooked on reasons and rules about not having the right set up which leads them to chronically avoid; others struggle with boredom when thinking of a task; others avoid tasks that are difficult for the most part. For example:

- Kara spends the whole morning vacuuming instead of doing her taxes.
- Jimmy spends the whole day planning his next vacation to Hawaii instead of calling his medical insurance to fix a bill.

- Jane gets ready to return unused items to the store, but as soon as she's getting ready to do so, she feels embarrassed about others seeing her.
- Joao knows he needs to register his new car and thinks that "there is time, I don't need to do it today."

Do any of these thoughts resonate with you?

The way you put things off and what you procrastinate may look completely different than the way another person does, yet the psychological drivers are the same for everyone.

The pattern of procrastinating behaviors can slip into a single area of your life or a combination of them; you may be in the habit of not replying to emails for weeks in a row but immediately take care of washing dirty dishes, even though you dislike this activity very much.

Let's spend some time examining in detail what typically happens when you find yourself procrastinating.

TRACING THE PATH OF PROCRASTINATION IN YOUR LIFE

To better understand your procrastinating behaviors, think about the contexts or settings where they're most likely to happen; you may find that you struggle most with putting off decisions in your personal life but are fine at work, or vice versa.

In the next activity, you'll reflect on which area or areas of your life are most likely to be affected by procrastinating behaviors.

ACTIVITY: Where does procrastination show up in your life?

Think about each one of the following areas of your life and the specific activities you have been putting off over the last three months.

Please be as specific as possible. Don't worry about how big or small the activity is.

The goal of this exercise is to take a big-picture view and map out areas where you're currently procrastinating.

- Friendships: What visits, trips, gatherings, or activities to stay in touch with others have you been putting off in your relationships with friends?

  ....
  ....
  ....
  ....

- Family relationships: If you have a partner or are a parent, does procrastination affect how you act in those roles?

  ....
  ....
  ....
  ....

- Personal wellness/health: What are the health-related tasks—exercising, medical appointments, shopping, personal hygiene—you have been dreading?

  ....
  ....
  ....
  ....

- Personal financial: Are there bills, contracts, taxes, banking matters, retirement funds, or other financial responsibilities that you have been avoiding?

  ....

  ....

  ....

  ....

- Leisure: What are the hobbies, new activities, or sports you would have liked to start but ended up putting off?

  ....

  ....

  ....

  ....

- House chores: Do you tend to put off shopping, calling a contractor, unpacking, minor repairs, or other day-to-day chores at home?

  ....

  ....

  ....

  ....

- Work: What are the meetings, initiatives, classes, emails, reports, submissions, or other responsibilities you have been ignoring intentionally?

  ....

. . . .

. . . .

. . . .

- School or professional training: Are there any registrations, papers, exams, living arrangements, or classes on your radar you have chosen to avoid?

. . . .

. . . .

. . . .

. . . .

- Spiritual life: What services, practices, or rituals have you been thinking about but not acted upon?

. . . .

. . . .

. . . .

. . . .

- Other areas of your life:

. . . .

. . . .

. . . .

. . . .

What came up for you when writing down your responses? Did you notice any push to distract yourself from it, criticize yourself, hide, or power through it so you can easily say it's done? Please take a deep breath; this is an exercise of awareness; no need to criticize yourself at this moment. What are the areas of life that are affected by procrastination?

My appreciation to you for completing this activity and seeing firsthand the many colors, shapes, and sizes of procrastinating behaviors in your life. It's courageous of you to step back and map all those behaviors out where they occur.

PROCRASTINATION AND OTHER MENTAL HEALTH STRUGGLES

When my clients start digging into what areas of their lives are being affected by procrastinating behaviors, they often tell me, "I'm procrastinating because I'm depressed," or "It's my ADHD." These comments make so much sense because problematic procrastination rarely shows up in isolation.

To make a real change in your life and start getting things done, it is important to understand how procrastinating behaviors are different than or concurrent with other struggles.

Productive procrastination

Sometimes procrastination gives the illusion of productivity because you accomplish tasks—just not whatever you're putting off and avoiding. This is called productive procrastination.

Sam has decided to quit his job as a customer service representative at a sports equipment company after four years with no raise or change in duties. Every day, he dealt with the same questions and complaints over and over, an overwhelming number of administrative processes, tons of paperwork, and no power to make any changes in the product or logistical procedures of the company.

The standard two weeks of vacation limited Sam's time availability to take long road trips and explore new cities, one of his favorite hobbies. Sam discussed his decision with his partner and agreed to send his letter of resignation in January.

While sitting in the white leather chair in his cubicle, Sam opens his laptop, logs directly on to his work email, selects the option "compose," and then types in the subject, "resignation." He immediately feels that "it's not the right moment, I'm not feeling articulate enough." Then, he looks at the 23 emails that have arrived in his inbox and jumps into replying to them. Sam answers questions about a new membership program, questions about how to request for vacation from a new coach, scheduling matters for the electrician who needs to repair the light in the main fitness studio, the location for the next company retreat, and others. After an hour and 45 minutes, he feels satisfied when he sees only five emails in his inbox. He walks away to grab a glass of water and with a smile on his face, thinks, "my goodness, glad I took care of the emails right away."

By April, despite Sam's strong desire to quit his job, he has not communicated his decision to resign to his manager.

When thinking about procrastination, most people are familiar with the action of postponing intentionally important activities and replacing them with fun ones, like playing video games instead of doing homework. Yet often people put off important and even high-priority projects by replacing them with other tasks, which may also be important but are less triggering and easier to accomplish. They rationalize that they did accomplish something—even if it wasn't what they intended to do or needed to do.

If you engage in productive productivity, you're not alone. In a study conducted by Westgate and colleagues (2017) among 1066 college students, they found that:

- 50.69 percent of them reported postponing academic tasks by focusing on other academic tasks
- 40.04 percent procrastinated by engaging in productive tasks that were non-academic, such as cleaning their room, doing the dishes, or exercising
- 44.02 percent procrastinated by engaging in more pleasurable activities like checking Facebook, watching television, socializing with friends, etc.

It looks like college students are masters of productive procrastination. What about you?

Procrastination and perfectionism

I have worked with clients who struggle with both perfectionism and procrastination. This combination is quite common, but it's important to distinguish when they are related and when they are not.

Perfectionistic, high-achieving, and striving actions are caused by the following psychological processes:

- excessive worry and anxiety about making mistakes
- intense fears of failing or being considered a failure
- high standards for yourself or others about yours or others' performance in different areas in your life
- a sense of self defined by accomplishments and failures.

The interaction of these core psychological drivers leads a person to engage in overworking and/or underworking actions. Overworking behaviors might include searching endlessly for information before making a decision, striving to be meticulous at all times, excessive list-making, overpreparing, or constantly overanalyzing. On the other hand, underworking behaviors include procrastinating, not finishing a project, avoiding activities that you fear you won't perform well, minimizing downtime, or refusing to do anything that you think could prove you're a failure.

At its core, perfectionism is fueled by a deep fear of failure or being seen as a failure; as a result, you work hard to protect yourself from this fear becoming a reality.

Now, as you learned in Chapter 1, a pattern of procrastination is driven by:

1. Non-acceptance of difficult emotions.
2. Going along with reasons.
3. Adherence to self-imposed rules.
4. Attachment to self-doubtful thoughts.
5. Proneness to impulsive feeling-based and short-term choices.
6. Disconnection from personal values.

While the psychological factors that lead someone to procrastinate or engage in perfectionist actions might look similar—both involve struggles with particular ways of thinking and emotional avoidance—they're also quite different.

A key distinction between perfectionism and procrastination is that when people develop perfectionistic behaviors they're primarily preoccupied with failing or being a failure. However—here is an important difference—when people fall into a procrastination, they may or may not be worried about failing or being perceived as a failure; instead, they might be consumed by other emotional states, like boredom, sadness, worry, stress, or embarrassment and hold on to different types of reasons.

If someone puts a project off because they think "it's not ready, it's not good enough, it's not right" and is afraid of failing, it doesn't automatically mean that this person is struggling with perfectionism. While that might be an easy assumption to make, it is important to look at other examples or other difficult moments this person deals with in their life to assess the main psychological drivers behind them.

I have worked with perfectionists who struggle with procrastination because their fear of being a failure pushes them to intentionally put things off; I have not seen procrastinators who are perfectionists.

The skills in this workbook are focused on problematic procrastinating actions. If you're struggling with both perfectionism and procrastination, some of the skills from this workbook will help you, but you will also benefit from learning additional skills to tackle the fear of failure directly.

I encourage you to explore my online class, ACT beyond Perfectionism, where you can learn how to harness the power of perfectionistic actions without losing or hurting your relationships (https://courses.thisisdoctorz.com).

Procrastination and Attention Deficit Hyperactivity Disorder (ADHD)

We all remember times when we jumped from one topic into another in a conversation, got easily distracted, struggled to manage time, or jumped in a car and ended up in a different destination than the planned one. Sometimes people refer to those kind of actions as "It's my ADHD." Even though this term is used colloquially, it's misleading and underestimates the real struggles that people with ADHD experience; many adults struggling with ADHD don't receive an accurate diagnosis or effective treatment until they have suffered for years or even decades.

ADHD is a neurodevelopmental disorder characterized by inattention, impulsivity, and hyperactivity. Another way of thinking about ADHD is as dysregulation of attention; yes, people with ADHD have difficulty paying attention, but not because they lack attention, it's the opposite. They have an abundance of attention, and often pay attention to everything at once, to the point that they lose track of what's important in a given moment.

The intersection of ADHD and procrastinating behaviors has been frequently noted in many studies (Ramsay 2020). Adults with ADHD struggle with finding the motivation to get things done and sustain their attention on a task; putting things off becomes a coping strategy to avoid dealing with the stress of the moment. Most people dealing with ADHD end up with a graveyard of partially finished projects, abandoned hobbies, stacks of notes, unused planners, and unfinished books with few marked-up pages.

If this description feels familiar to you or you already know that you're dealing with ADHD, I encourage you to find an experienced psychologist to evaluate your individual situation and recommend next steps.

Due to the huge overlap between ADHD and procrastination, the strategies, skills, and activities are likely to help you, especially if you're wrestling with a long history of not getting things done and putting things off.

Procrastination and depression

Let's start by distinguishing low mood from depression; we all experience the blues or low mood from time to time. Sometimes it can be triggered by external events—your pet passed away, you lose your job, you are going through a breakup, or struggling at work, to name a few events; other times, you wake up, open your eyes and you feel down without any clear cause.

Depression is a bio-psycho-social struggle that can be driven by a chemical imbalance, emotional situations, or a combination. Typical ongoing symptoms include:

- feeling sad, empty, hopeless, tearful and slowed down for most of the day
- loss of interest or pleasure in activities for most of the day or nearly every day
- decreased appetite
- sleeping difficulties
- loss of energy or feeling fatigued
- feelings of worthlessness
- difficulties concentrating
- some people experience recurrent thoughts of death.

If you're concerned that you may be, or know that you are, dealing with chronic depression, a major depressive episode, or suicidal thoughts, I encourage you to seek support from a mental health provider who specializes in mood struggles.

Depression can lead people to engage in procrastinating behaviors. However, it's also possible that a repetitive pattern of procrastinating actions can lead you to feel down, disconnected, isolated, and without any hope that you can do better.

If procrastinating behaviors and their effects are a root cause of your depression, addressing procrastination may help with depressive symptoms. Working through this book can help you tackle internal experiences that are keeping your mood low, hopeless, and perpetuating procrastination.

Procrastination and emotion regulation difficulties

Emotion regulation difficulties are usually associated with borderline personality disorder (BPD). I think of emotion regulation problems as super-feeling problems. It is a struggle that is not exclusive to people dealing with BPD but coexists with other types of suffering (anxiety, eating problems, substance abuse, body image concerns, and others).

Super-feelers have an emotion switch that turns on and off; they feel too much, too quick, and act too soon. Their emotions run their behaviors 24/7, with no vacations and no holidays. When they feel sad, they're pulverized with sadness; when they feel anxious, they're crushed with anxiety; when they feel guilty, they're flooded with guilt.

They experience their emotions quickly and intensely; they believe every thought, interpretation, or hypothesis that comes into their mind and do exactly what the emotion tells them to do. Later on, they regret their actions because they get hurt and the people they care about get hurt too.

If you're a super-feeler, I highly recommend you get and practice the skills from my previous book, *Escaping the Emotional Roller Coaster* (2018), and search for a provider that specializes in emotion regulation challenges.

Some researchers, such as Sirois (2023), conceptualize procrastination as an emotion regulation struggle; procrastination is, at a general level, a problem driven by difficulties regulating your responses to uncomfortable emotional states. But, as you recall from Chapter 1, in addition to struggling with emotions, other psychological processes cause you to chronically put things off; therefore, learning to deal with yucky feelings is necessary, and not enough. You also need other skills to overcome the procrastination habit.

If you're a super-feeler who also struggles with procrastinating behaviors, you grabbed the right book.

WRAPPING UP

You have learned how procrastination intertwines with other struggles like emotional regulation difficulties, ADHD, and depression; we also carefully explored the concept of productive procrastination as well as the similarities and differences between perfectionism and procrastination.

The next chapters will give you the tools you need to overcome your proneness to put your life off, so you can fully focus on what's most important to you. No matter how long you have been procrastinating, with patience and practice, you can begin building the life you have been waiting for.

CHAPTER 3

FINDING THE COMPASS OF YOUR LIFE

The most precious resource in our lives is time. We have a finite amount of time to live, be who we want to be, and show our love to all the people who matter to us. If we think of life as a bank account, we're making withdrawals every single minute, and there is no way to deposit more!

Many authors from different disciplines (from Seneca's philosophical reflections in *On the Shortness of Life* to insights founds in poetry, novels, comedies, and science fiction films like *Bill and Ted's Excellent Adventure*) have explored the concept of our limited time on earth. In his bestseller, *Four Thousand Weeks: Time Management for Mortals* (2021), Oliver Burkeman reminds us of a truth we all face and often forget: What are we going to do with our limited time on earth?

How would you answer this question?

What do you do with your time from the moment you open your eyes to the moment you fall asleep on an average day of your week?

. . . .

. . . .

. . . .

. . . .

. . . .

. . . .

. . . .

. . . .

How are you investing your time?

As you go through your day, you probably find yourself juggling all kinds of activities across different areas of your life. It's likely that you fully attend to some tasks, half-finish others, and choose to put things off completely.

When you regularly delay a task, you're not just putting a project off, you're also putting your life off. Procrastinating behaviors keep you pushing away your goals, relationships, and opportunities to experience joy, happiness, and purpose. And as time slips by, it's easy to lose sight of what truly matters to you.

Let me ask you:

- Why waste your life?
- Why run away from what matters to you?
- Why continue making choices that make it harder for you to be who you want to be?

Neglecting what truly matters to you over time is an underlying psychological process that fuels procrastinating patterns. This chapter is about reconnecting with what's genuinely important to you, finding your compass, and focusing on what you want your life to stand for!

No matter how long you've been trapped in a pattern of not getting things done, you're wired to seek meaning and purpose every day you are alive.

ART OF BECOMING

Getting better at time management, pairing up with an accountability partner, setting alarms, or doing any other clichéd advice you have heard about to discontinue all those procrastinating behaviors are not enough to build a life you're proud of.

It's not one single action, app, or habit, or a collection of them that will get you to live a rich life. It's about coming back to what makes you feel alive, gives you purpose, and brings joy in your everyday life.

Let's do a brief exercise.

ACTIVITY: Celebrating your birthday party

I was having dinner with my 101-year-old great-great aunt, Tia Fibi, and chatting about her recent birthday party. She looked at me and said in a soft voice in Spanish, "Hijita, la fiesta fue muy bonita. Todos estaban ahi; todos me abrazaron; cantamos, comimos, bailamos un poquito, ya no puedo bailar mucho, y me dijeron cosas bonitas de nuestros tiempo juntos." [My little daughter, it was a sweet party; everyone was there; everyone hugged me. We sang, ate, danced a bit—I cannot dance much these days, and they told me nice things about our times together.]

Imagine that it's your 101st birthday party and you're surrounded by the people you love and cherish in life. One by one, they share a few words about you, stories, anecdotes, what they appreciate about you, what they admire about you, and what you mean to them. In an ideal world, where you have lived your life as it matters to you, what would you like them to say about you?

• Parents

. . . .

. . . .

. . . .

- Siblings

. . . .

. . . .

. . . .

- Partner/Spouse

. . . .

. . . .

. . . .

- Children

. . . .

. . . .

. . . .

- Friends

. . . .

. . . .

. . . .

- Colleagues/Peers

. . . .

· ·

· ·

After completing this exercise, read your responses and check if any themes emerged. Write those themes below:

· ·

· ·

· ·

· ·

· ·

· ·

· ·

· ·

· ·

Imagine for a moment how it could be for you if every day of your life you showed up to others and yourself in a way that matters to you, in a way that makes you proud of who you are.

Some of you may be saying, "Yeah, yeah, yeah, I know I need to be mindful, but it's not my thing." If so, let's touch base about it.

There is a misconception in pop psychology that the pursuit of a meaningful life is something like an esoteric pursuit, or that you have to meditate every day, stay in a monastery, travel to Tibet or India, or attend hundreds of dharma talks. I'm sure I could write a whole chapter focused on all those misconceptions about finding meaning in life.

Living a life worth living may or may not include some of those pursuits, but it's not just that. Living a purposeful life is freely choosing who you want to be, what's important to you, and capitalizing on those sources of meaning that are around you wherever you go.

You don't need necessarily to travel to Bolivia to find purpose in your life, you don't need to do a ten-day silent retreat (of course, it's okay to take a spiritual journey if you want to).

The point I'm trying to make is that no matter how much you have been putting things off, or wherever you are in life, every moment you're breathing you have an opportunity to behave as if it's important to you, to do what adds purpose to your day, and to enrich the quality of your connections with others and yourself.

You're the only one that can make those choices to embrace those qualities as if you're building the foundation of your life.

THE POWER OF MEANINGFUL LIVING

Within ACT, we think of those personal qualities you want to live by, be known by, and be remembered by as your personal values.

I'm aware it's very trendy these days to talk about values, but a uniqueness in the ACT approach is to think of your values as patterns of ongoing action you can take to be the person you want to be (Hayes *et al.* 2006, p.16).

In other words, we think of your values as verbs; as long as you're alive, you always have an opportunity to intentionally choose who you want to be, no matter how old you are, what you're doing, where you are, or who you're with.

Values are your heart's deepest desires for how you want to behave—now and in the future—guiding the direction you want to take.

Think for a moment of Richard and Abdul.

Richard cares deeply about eating healthily so he picks up fresh produce every week, cooks five out of seven evenings, and avoids eating processed food. Richard's value of "eating healthily" is never finished or completed because he can always translate his value into more actions.

For Abdul, it is very important to "be a present father" with his teenage daughters, so at dinner every evening, he makes sure to ask them what was difficult or fun in their days, drives them to their sports activities on Sundays, and makes a point of listening to them before jumping into advice-giving mode.

Goals or activities can be checked off as completed, but your values can't. It's like your values are always in the present, in the here-and-now, and the actions that come along are in the future and need to be completed.

Richard can mark off "cooking five meals a week, getting fresh produce from the market on Wednesday, growing tomatoes in his backyard, and preparing a new vegan recipe every Friday" as completed goals.

As Abdul's daughters grow, he could add new activities with his daughters, let go of others, or change the schedule for them, but all of them are working toward his value of "being an engaged father."

Richard and Abdul are taking action and working toward their goals, focusing on what really matters to them concerning their health and parenting, respectively; they're never eveeeeeeeeeeer done living out their values.

At times, people confuse values with feelings or emotional avoidance. You can listen to Episode 23, "Dr. Z. on Values," in the podcast Playing-it-Safe (Zurita Ona 2021), which will help you to get crystal clear about what values are and what they are not.

The next activity will help you further clarify your personal values. Even if you already have a good sense of what matters to you in certain areas of your life, I still invite you to give it a try. It doesn't hurt to reassess how you want to behave, and how you want to treat yourself and the world around you.

ACTIVITY: Choosing your values

Listed below are personal qualities that most people value. Choose the ones that are important to you.

Accountability	Consistency	Flexibility
Adventure	Contribution	Forgiveness
Authenticity	Cooperation	Freedom
Balance	Courage	Generosity
Belonging	Creativity	Genuineness
Bravery	Curiosity	Gratitude
Calmness	Dependability	Harmony
Caring	Determination	Helpfulness
Charity	Devotion	Honesty
Collaboration	Dignity	Humility
Commitment	Discipline	Humor
Compassion	Empathy	Inclusivity
Competence	Equality	Independence
Confidence	Excellence	Influence
Connection	Fairness	Ingenuity

Innovation	Optimism	Restraint
Integrity	Patience	Sensitivity
Intelligence	Peace	Service
Intuition	Perseverance	Simplicity
Justice	Playfulness	Sincerity
Kindness	Practicality	Support
Knowledge	Presence	Thankfulness
Learning	Productivity	Tolerance
Loyalty	Purpose	Trust
Mindfulness	Reliability	Understanding
Modesty	Respect	Warmth
Open-mindedness	Responsibility	Wisdom

Would you add other values or life principles you want to stand up for?

. . . .

. . . .

. . . .

. . . .

. . . .

. . . .

. . . .

Let's dive deeper into another values clarification exercise to connect with your heart's deepest desires.

ACTIVITY: Reflecting on what matters in your everyday life

Reflect on the questions below and jot down your responses:

If you only had 24 hours to be alive, what would you do and who would you spend them with? What are the personal qualities you would like to show up in the world in those 24 hours?

. . . .

. . . .

. . . .

. . . .

When you look at the pain you feel because of procrastinating behaviors, what is that pain showing you about what truly matters to you?

. . . .

. . . .

. . . .

. . . .

What do you want your epitaph to say?

. . . .

. . . .

. . . .

. . . .

What brings you a sense of vitality in your life or a sense of being alive—no matter how small or big it is—that you would choose to do it again and again?

. . . .

. . . .

. . . .

. . . .

Research shows that committing to living meaningfully is essential for your overall well-being. For instance, a study led by Jennifer Aaker and colleagues at Stanford Graduate School of Business found that while pursuing happiness—a feeling—is important, embedding your actions with meaning leads you to deeper, more sustained well-being and profound fulfillment (Baumeister *et al.* 2013).

ACTIVITY: Connecting with your values

Below you will see areas of life that most people value; you may resonate more with certain areas than others. Based on the different values exploration activities you have completed, write down your personal values for each area that is important to you.

It's okay to skip the areas that don't apply to you. Your values in one area may overlap with others so don't stress about getting it perfect. This exercise is not about perfectly defining what's truly important to you; it's more about bringing to the forefront what you want your life to stand for.

- Family relationships

. . . .

....

....

- Friendships

....

....

....

- Marriage/couples/romantic relationships

....

....

....

- Parenting

....

....

....

- Career/education

....

....

....

- Spirituality

....

· ·

· ·

• Recreation

· ·

· ·

· ·

• Community

· ·

· ·

· ·

• Well-being/Physical health

· ·

· ·

· ·

When you're clear about what truly matters to you, it's like having a personal compass that helps you spot when you're moving toward the life you want or drifting away from it. Your values can guide you through those moments when procrastination sneaks in, giving you the chance to stay on course or get sidetracked. The choice is always yours.

Please keep in mind that no one can guarantee any outcomes or what will happen when you behave according to what matters to you. You can, of course, do things that increase your chances of reaching specific outcomes, but no one can guarantee any of it.

You may be thinking, "but I want the outcomes," and trust me, I get it. I'll dive more into goals and outcomes in Chapter 6, Aligning Your Choosing with Your Being.

For now, I encourage you to intentionally slow down and observe how it feels to live your values when you make a values-based choice. Don't wait for a challenging situation to present itself to you; instead, keep your eyes open for opportunities to sprinkle your values into whatever you're doing or saying.

I can genuinely tell you that when I started asking myself, "What's really, really, really important to me in the big picture?"—whether during difficult conversations, approaching tough choices, or deciding how to manage my time—and then made decisions aligned with my values, I felt a unique sense of aliveness and inner peace.

Embracing my values showed me how to be truthful to myself; I hope the same for you!

STAYING TRUE TO YOUR VALUES

Raj is very scared about having a panic attack; he becomes petrified when having shortness of breath, a racing heartbeat, or strong tingling sensations in his legs. Because of this fear, Raj has been avoiding grocery shopping, taking his kids to school, attending social gatherings, playing tennis, walking his dogs, or going out with his wife.

He never knows when a panic attack will strike, so he's always on guard, meticulously scanning to the "t" his physical sensations and anything that triggers them. Raj's mind often conjures thoughts like, "Why is this happening to me? I'm going to die. I'm going to have a heart attack; I'm going crazy; I shouldn't leave my house; it's not safe."

When discussing what truly matters to him as a father and husband, he said, "I don't want my life to be about always being on guard, waiting for the next panic attack to come. I want to be present with my kids and wife. I want to be part of their life. I don't want to be an absent father or husband, but one that they can talk to, share about their days, laugh together, take weekend road trips, or eat ice-cream on a Sunday."

Being clear about your values is half the battle in breaking procrastinating habits and building the life you want to live; engaging in values-based actions is the other half. Without values-based actions you're living reactively, randomly, and letting life pass by you by.

Making values-based moves is not easy-peasy or blissful all the time because you cannot tackle a project without experiencing internal discomfort. Raj cannot be the present and engaged father and husband he aspires to be without experiencing those scary physical sensations, fears about having a panic attack, and the discomfort that comes when doing the things he wants to do with his family. There will be highs and lows, and everything in between when building a well-lived life.

As you start deliberately taking values-based steps in life, you can expect your mind to come up with tricky and distracting thoughts.

Don't be surprised when that happens!

Your mind will push you in the direction of avoidance, distraction, postponement, and basically a detour from who you want to be.

There are two particular thoughts you want to pay attention to:

TRICKY THOUGHT: "IT'S TOO LATE AND IT'S TOO MUCH!"

Zach found that the more he learned about why he procrastinates and thought of his values, the more he felt frustrated with himself. He felt that he had wasted his life and that it was too late to change!

Is that you?

- Do you feel that it's impossible to make a shift now given all the stuff you have put off?
- Do you find yourself thinking that it's too late to break your procrastinating habits?
- Do you feel ashamed for past choices you have made postponing things over and over?

It's possible that the more you see the many ways you have been procrastinating, the more you get frustrated and disappointed with yourself; and the more you feel that gap between the life you want to live and the life you're living, because of the lack of taking care of things, the more you feel overwhelmed and hopeless.

This gap can be painful, and it may feel like the only solution in front of you is to give up, criticize yourself, or keep doing what you have been doing up to this point.

The reality is that changing the pattern of procrastination is not easy or instantaneous under any circumstances; it's hard, painful, and unfamiliar.

I'm sorry about this uncomfortable moment. But it's also not impossible for you to make a shift in your life.

You're reading these pages because you want to do things differently. This is a moment for you to choose between continue engaging in the same old postponing habits and behaving in new ways toward a life you're proud of.

Press your feet firmly against the floor, slow down your breathing, and anchor yourself in this moment. Do your best to continue with the next section with an open attitude and honoring the choice you have made already when you first started working on this workbook.

A touch of forgiveness

Before you jump to conclusions about the word "forgiveness," let's be on the same page about what it means and how it can be helpful to you.

Forgiveness or self-forgiveness does not mean giving yourself a free pass or ignoring the consequences of your procrastinating actions.

Forgiveness is a personal decision to pause from holding anger, bitterness, resentment, frustrations, or grudges toward yourself. You cannot get rid of those feelings unless you acknowledge them first. That's why forgiveness is often more difficult than it sounds to many people.

A study conducted by Wohl and colleagues (2010) suggested that students who forgave themselves for their procrastinating behaviors on a first exam experienced less uncomfortable emotions and were more motivated to prepare for a second test. In contrast, students who didn't forgive themselves for procrastinating on studying for the first test felt worse and procrastinated again on studying for the second test.

Noticing those self-criticizing tendencies and overwhelming feelings without going along with them and, instead, intentionally forgiving yourself will allow you to spend your emotional energy on approaching what's important to you, get things done, and break the shackles of procrastination.

The activities below will guide you to shift from getting stuck with the thoughts, "It's too much, can't do it" to self-forgiveness. Be sure to complete each exercise without skipping any, as they build on one another and they're meant to be done in sequence.

ACTIVITY: Acknowledging your choices

Jot down a few sentences acknowledging that it was your choice to procrastinate on a particular activity without blaming yourself or finding external sources as the cause of your choices.

. . . .

. . . .

. . . .

. . . .

. . . .

Next, notice any feelings that show up, such as an urge to judge yourself or to distract yourself from these feelings, and say, "Here is [name of the feeling]."

. . . .

. . . .

. . . .

. . . .

. . . .

Ask yourself, is there anything to learn from this situation? What would you do differently next time? Write down your response below.

. . . .

. . . .

. . . .

. . . .

. . . .

You cannot practice self-forgiveness without taking ownership of the choices you made when postponing things. Notice your internal experience as you acknowledge your past decisions, and reflect on what changes you need to make in the future toward the life that you want to nourish.

You're not alone, we all have been there!

Now, let me walk you through an experiential exercise focused on self-forgiveness.

ACTIVITY: Practicing a self-forgiveness meditation

For this exercise, read the directions below first, then get a recording device, record the directions slowly, and then listen to them as you do the exercise.

1. Choose a memory of a procrastinating behavior that is somewhat painful but not too overwhelming. It's best to start with a memory that is mildly distressing since you're just beginning to practice forgiveness.

2. After selecting the procrastinating memory you wish to work on, sit down and ground yourself: Press your feet firmly against the floor, imagining yourself as the trunk of a strong tree.

3. Take slow and deep breaths. Do your best to fill your belly with air, and then completely release the air through your nose.

4. Bring into your mind the procrastinating memory you have chosen to work on as clearly as possible. See if you can visualize all the characteristics of that painful memory, such as the colors, sounds, location, and time of day. Try to even hear the words that were said during that particular painful scene.

5. While holding this memory in mind, shift the focus of your attention to your body and see if you can notice any sensations you may be having at this moment.

6. Slowly and with intention, gently name the emotion that is coming along with this procrastinating memory. Can you make room for it? Can you notice the uniqueness of this emotion? Describe this emotion to yourself for what it is, an emotion; notice how it feels in your body, whether it's moving or not.

    If there are any judgments about this exercise, such as "good" or "bad," kindly name them as judgments. If anger or resentment shows up, see if you can notice how anger or resentment feels in your body. What type of sensation shows up? What's the quality of these sensations? Notice if there is any wish to push the anger, resentment, or any other emotion away.

Is your pain coming from the event itself or from holding on to the memory of the procrastinating event? Is it possible that the memory of the procrastinating event is the trigger for your pain? See if you can notice the pain that comes from holding on to this memory, dwelling on it, and replaying it over and over. The harder you hold on to it, the more waves of pain you will go through.

See if you can become curious about other emotions or sensations that are showing up in this exercise as they come and go. Are you willing to notice how your emotions shift while you continue to work on this painful procrastinating memory? Is the same emotion present? Is it a different one? Is the emotion as intense as the first one you recalled, or does it have a different intensity now? Can you simply notice the shift from one emotion into another, from the beginning of the exercise to this point? Can you notice the shift in physical sensations from the beginning of the exercise to now?

7. Offer yourself forgiveness by saying a gentle, forgiving phrase for the choice you made to put things off, intentionally or unintentionally, wittingly or unwittingly. Notice how it feels to offer yourself forgiveness without hours of criticizing yourself and without judging yourself for letting it go or blaming yourself.

8. Slowly bring your attention back to your breathing and stay with it for a while. Let your emotions settle into the spaciousness of your breath and awareness.

Take your time to reflect on these questions:

- What's the payoff for forgiving myself in this moment?
- Is there something for me to learn from letting go of my resentment toward myself?

Self-forgiveness is a skill to deal with the urge to blame yourself and the feeling that change is impossible; you can always go back to this exercise as many times as needed.

Another block from living your values that I have heard from my clients is the...

TRICKY THOUGHT: "WHAT'S THE POINT?"

Alex wondered, "What's the point in working on that boring report? I hate wasting my time on it. I don't care about history and don't have any intention to become a historian or pursue any career that involves history. It's not related to my values. So, why do I need to care about it?"

- How often do you find yourself, like Alex, struggling to find meaning in tasks that feel pointless, boring, and annoying?
- How often do you feel burdened by obligations that seem irrelevant to you?
- Do you often struggle to find purpose in seemingly simple tasks?

It makes sense that if you don't find something important or relevant to you, you won't get it done and you will postpone it to the best of your abilities. Who wouldn't? Who wants to complete tasks that you don't see as related to your values?

I'm sure that there are many tasks that when you look at them, don't energize you and it feels that it's almost impossible to see their usefulness in your life; just like Alex felt when looking at a report he needed to write and had been postponing it for four months.

Many people struggling with procrastinating behaviors, like Alex, often encounter tasks that don't resonate with their values and feel uninteresting at first glance. In those moments, of course, it's tempting to avoid the discomfort these tasks bring by quickly finding reasons to put them off, like listening to the thought, "What's the point of this project?"

From a place of honesty, I can tell you that it's hard for me to see the benefits of interrupting my morning to go to the store, searching through endless shelves for a light bulb, feeling like an idiot, trying to figure out the subtle differences between each type of light bulb, waiting in line for at least 30 minutes, and then driving back home. All just for a light bulb!

It feels like a colossal task that doesn't add anything to my life. But, by taking care of that mundane task, I take care of my well-being. Having a comfortable setting at home—with proper light—helps me to be grounded and replenish my energy.

Let's try something different to stop quickly dismissing the impact of all those mundane tasks in your life and stop feeding into procrastination.

ACTIVITY: Looking beyond mundane tasks

Think about one activity that is too ordinary, simplistic, or an activity that you don't see as worthy of your time, and jot it down below.

....

....

Answer the following questions:

- How does completing each step of this task help your well-being in the long run?

....

· ·

- What long-term goals does this task move you toward?

· ·

· ·

- How would this project take you closer to who you want to be in future?

· ·

· ·

What came up for you when looking at how that particular task could contribute to the life you want to build?

When you intentionally slow down and look beyond the call you have to make, the spreadsheet you have to work on, the bill you have to pay, the upgrade you need to your cell phone, or the meeting you need to arrange with your manager, that's when you need to open your eyes to your personal values.

Building a life you love requires purposeful, intentional, and consistent actions; it also requires that you show up to those tedious, boring, and annoying tasks as they come your way while your mind tells you, "What's the point?"

When your mind tells you, "What's the point of [name an activity your mind is prone to avoid]," you need to go back to your values, to what truly matters to you, again and again, and ask yourself the questions from the last activity.

Here is another exercise to tackle those tasks that seem irrelevant.

ACTIVITY: Turning mundane tasks into social opportunities

Lyubomirsky and colleagues (2005) found that social connection is one of the strongest predictors of happiness and well-being. When looking at the tasks that seem irrelevant at first—even though your mind pushes you to postpone them—turn those moments into opportunities for connection and support.

Here are some questions for you to consider:

- How would this task help you to build a life worth living in the future?

  ....

  ....

- Who can you connect with while doing this task?

  ....

  ....

- How can you make this task more enjoyable by involving others?

  ....

  ....

  ....

- How can this task serve you as an opportunity to strengthen your relationships?

  ....

  ....

  ....

Give it a try!

WRAPPING UP

Congratulations on spending time on the most important activities of your life: clarifying what truly matters to you!

When you engage over and over in values-guided behaviors, you become who you want to be without being dominated by procrastinating behaviors.

Moving forward, when getting stuck, ask yourself, if I do x does it bring me closer to or further away from building the life I want to build in the long run?

You're fully capable of making values-based choices.

CHAPTER 4

BE GOOD TO YOURSELF!

Imagine you're walking in a forest or an open field, and all of a sudden you feel a sharp pain in your leg. When you look below your hip, you see you've been struck by an arrow. It's painful and you feel overwhelmed. You're surprised. You're shocked. Then, your mind starts yelling at you: "You idiot! You should've known better. What's wrong with you? How come you didn't see that arrow coming? Are you blind? Why did you allow this to happen? You're stupid. Others would have done better than you."

THE TALE OF TWO ARROWS

The first arrow is the pain you feel in your leg. It's an inevitable discomfort. The second arrow is, metaphorically speaking, your reaction to the first arrow. It's like you struck your leg with an arrow a second time. This is a popular parable in Buddhism called "The Tale of Two Arrows."

When your mind comes up with self-judging thoughts like, "Will I be able to do this? I'm not sure I'm smart enough to do this…" these thoughts are the first arrow and they are painful by nature. The ongoing criticism, self-judgment, shaming, comparison, and rumination are the second arrow that adds further suffering. Sound familiar?

I'm not saying that when you feel the first arrow you should pretend it didn't happen and think about your favorite snack. I'm suggesting there are other more effective ways of dealing with the unavoidable pain that comes with the first arrow.

In this chapter, we're going to dive into trying to understand how you relate to yourself, how the relationship with yourself works, and what you can do differently to overcome procrastination.

Here are two brief reflective questions for you:

How do you treat yourself when you identify as a procrastinator?

. . . .

. . . .

. . . .

. . . .

What do you think of yourself and your competence when ignoring tasks?

. . . .

. . . .

. . . .

. . . .

You may have noticed that, more often than not, you're hard on yourself.

Being hard on yourself and doubting yourself are core psychological processes that push you to put things off and maintain procrastinating habits over and over again (see Chapter 1 to review all the psychological processes that cause and reinforce procrastination).

If you're like the clients I work with, you quite likely feel intensely those self-doubting and critical thoughts that show up; then, naturally, you are reluctant to start anything or to continue with a project because your mind won't stop generating those thoughts. To manage those painful thoughts, you put tasks off. The challenge is that, after avoiding those tasks, you end up feeling worse about yourself and beating yourself up for hours.

ACTIVITY: What does your first arrow look like?

Think about a specific moment when your mind came up with those critical thoughts or doubts about your ability to do things; write them down as they show up in your mind.

. . . .

. . . .

. . . .

. . . .

What did you feel when seeing those thoughts written down?

. . . .

. . . .

. . . .

. . . .

If the thoughts about yourself focus primarily on being a failure, I encourage you to keep in mind the section "Procrastination and perfectionism" from Chapter 2 and take a look at the resources mentioned there.

Most of my clients feel ashamed, frustrated, or angry with themselves when recognizing those first arrow thoughts, as if those thoughts define their identity.

Do you relate to those feelings of shame?

SHAME: A COMMON FIRST ARROW

Etymologically speaking, the word shame comes from the Latin word "to cover." At a psychological level, shame is seen as a social emotion.

When we feel ashamed, we do exactly what the origins of the word convey: we hide, conceal, and disconnect from any situation or people that could expose the bad, broken, and defective parts we carry within ourselves. We don't feel ashamed in isolation but in relation to others; we feel we're less than people around us.

Though shame might make you squirm, it's an emotion that has accompanied us since the beginning of humanity. Think about it: the cavemen and cavewomen needed to protect themselves from breaking group rules, feeling rejected by others, segregation, and so on, so they could continue being part of the group. Otherwise, they would die. If they did something harmful to others, such as not bringing enough food or failing to protect the tribe, they would feel ashamed and would be rejected from the group. So, shame evolved as a feeling that contributed to protecting us from social rejection, ostracism, and being shunned.

Though it's not the easiest thing to accept, shame is just another emotion, not good or bad on its own, just a feeling passing through. How you respond to it in each moment is what truly shapes its impact on your life. When you act out of shame, you might do things that help you fit in, like holding back from lashing out in public, refraining from hurtful comments, or resisting the urge to take something that isn't yours. However, at other times, especially when dealing with procrastination, you may end up hiding from tasks, missing connections with others, or avoiding new hobbies which take you on a detour from being the person that you aspire to be.

That's why it is very important to check your responses to shame, your first arrow, and how you deal with it in any given moment.

ACTIVITY: How do you relate to shame?

Bring to mind a moment in which you felt ashamed. How does shame feel to you?

. . . .

. . . .

. . . .

. . . .

What do you notice in your body?

. . . .

. . . .

. . . .

. . . .

What do you do at that moment?

. . . .

. . . .

. . . .

. . . .

What do you do in the long term?

. . . .

. . . .

. . . .

. . . .

To get things done without hours of negative self-judgment, feeling trapped and hopeless, or the pain that comes from being harsh with yourself, you need to deal skillfully with shame and foster a workable relationship with yourself.

A NEW WAY

One powerful way to get better at managing those shameful feelings, self-criticism, and self-doubtful thoughts is to imagine your critical self as a separate entity, almost like an uninvited guest who keeps showing up.

The more vividly you can imagine your critical self, the easier it becomes to notice when it's taking over.

And while it might feel uneasy at first, the more you practice making room for those shameful thoughts and feelings without pushing them away, the better you get at having them instead of them having you.

The next two activities will help you to observe shame, your first arrow, as it happens to you.

ACTIVITY: Opening up to your critical self

Find a quiet place where you won't be bothered for ten minutes.

Close your eyes, start paying attention to your breathing and bring to mind a project, activity, or task you have been procrastinating over. Notice how it feels in your body to face that project: What self-doubting or critical thoughts appear in your mind?

. . . .

. . . .

. . . .

. . . .

. . . .

If those thoughts were a person, how would the person look and sound? What is this person asking you to do? Do your best to imagine this vividly, as if this person is right in front of you.

. . . .

. . . .

. . . .

. . . .

. . . .

Briefly describe the situation you visualized.

. . . .

. . . .

. . . .

. . . .

. . . .

Describe your critical self.

. . . .

....

....

....

....

How did it feel in your body to notice this critical self? Take a moment to describe what you notice in your body.

....

....

....

....

....

What did the critical self ask you to do?

....

....

....

....

....

If you were to give a name to this critical self, what would it be?

....

....

....

· ·

· ·

How was it for you to complete this exercise? Being human is very challenging at times. Rather than reacting in automatic pilot when your critical self shows up, you can get better at catching it in action.

ACTIVITY: Catching your critical self in action

Moving forward, I'd like to invite you to start noticing all the times your critical self shows up uninvited in your life. Your critical self can easily slip in when you're feeling down, when you make a mistake, or even when things are going well. The first step is to bring it into the light and acknowledge it—not with hostility or resistance as if it's your enemy, but with a sense of curiosity and even a bit of humor.

When your critical self pops up, this is what you need to do: Acknowledge it, all the way!

You can even greet it. You can say things like, "Hello, Mr. Critic, I see you're back" or "Hi, Mr. Critical, long time no see!"

You can also capture a theme from those critical thoughts, name them and greet them as such: "Hello, Mr. Not Good Enough," or, "Hi, Mr. Incompetent."

You can get creative with it too and give your critical self a playful name that captures their essence. For example:

- "Hello, Mr. Not Good Enough, I see you're here again."
- "Hi, Miss Incompetent, what's the urgent message this time?"
- "Oh, it's Mr. You'll Never Measure Up, haven't seen you in a while."

You can also be playful and imagine your critical self as a character with a ridiculous voice, like a grumpy parrot or a pesky mosquito buzzing in your ear.

The goal here isn't to argue with your critical self or try to make it go away, it's to become more aware of it and practice responding in a way that is a bit kinder, a bit softer and a bit less controlled by the old shameful, judgmental and self-doubtful scripts your mind comes up with.

If you're prone to self-attacking, do your best to acknowledge your critical self in some way. For example, a client of mine simply nods his head.

The more you practice, the more you'll notice that this critical voice isn't the whole of you; it's just a part of you, one that you can choose how to engage with.

Jot down how you would acknowledge your critical self when it appears in your life.

....

....

....

....

....

....

....

Next week when your critical self shows up make sure to notice how you deal with it or what you do.

....

....

....

....

....

. . . .

. . . .

Kudos to you for completing this activity! You have chosen to tune in to something that is uncomfortable and that you're naturally prone to avoid.

Look back at this exercise and see if there is a common pattern in your responses. Do you have go-to responses when those self-critical or self-doubting thoughts show up?

Let's continue with other exercises to foster a workable relationship with your critical self so you don't make things worse for yourself with a second arrow.

DEVELOPING A COMPASSIONATE RELATIONSHIP WITH YOURSELF

Most people are familiar with the importance of extending compassion to others:

- If a good friend of yours is going through a breakup or divorce, you probably show up for your friend with encouraging words, sympathy, and gentleness.
- If your pet gets sick, you quite likely pet him, feed him, spend time with him, hold him in your arms if possible, and make sure he has his meds, if needed.
- If you're walking down the street and see a stranger fall, you stop and check if they are okay.

You will do all kinds of things to show compassion to people who matter to you and also to strangers. When you're guided by your interpersonal values, you will show up for others as you want to be remembered by them.

Compassion for others is crucial. Self-compassion is also crucial in our relationship with ourselves, the life we want to build and when tackling our procrastinating habits. This workbook is not about how to never be critical toward yourself, but how to meet your critical self in ways that ease rather than inflame.

Self-compassion has nothing to do with being soft, self-serving, loose, weak, self-pitying, selfish, or self-centered.

Self-compassion is about caring for yourself and doing something for yourself when you're hurting or when something is upsetting to you.

WHAT IF I DON'T DESERVE SELF-COMPASSION?

I can hear you saying, "It's not for me to be self-compassionate; I don't deserve it. I mess up often, I'm lazy. Self-compassion is weak." But I can tell you right away that self-attacks won't take you far.

Many people are afraid that if they show themselves self-compassion, they will be less effective or successful, or they will become lazy. Other people believe that because they haven't experienced self-compassion, they don't have it within them. Rest assured that research doesn't support this idea.

For now, I want to encourage you to put your skepticism and self-attacks aside, write down all those thoughts about self-compassion not working for you at the edge of this page, and continue reading this chapter.

When encountering experiential activities in this chapter or the rest of the workbook, don't force yourself into them; instead, choose to participate with beginner's eyes. Ease yourself into new practices slowly and be kind to yourself.

Being good to ourselves is not new. It's something people have always done. Our ancestors developed three physiological systems that organized their behavior, helped them coexist with others, and kept them alive.

When cavemen and cavewomen were protecting themselves from menace and danger, their threat system was in action; their drive system was activated when they were motivated to find the resources and supplies needed to survive. When our ancestors needed to stay calm, rest, and appease themselves to feel safe, they relied on their soothing system (Gilbert 2009; Kolts 2016).

Even though you live in a very, very different environment from those early humans, evolution has shaped the way you scan for threats, seek resources, and soothe yourself using these same emotion-regulation systems as the cavemen and cavewomen.

When struggling with procrastination, it's quite likely you have learned to use your threat system to approach your critical self, negative thoughts, doubts about your competence, or the possibility of failure. So, you respond to those thoughts as a threat that must be eliminated, squashed, and controlled. You do that by attacking yourself.

Here's the caveat: You have the same predisposition as our ancestors to activate your soothing system when that self-critical voice shows up in your mind. You don't need to attack yourself with a second arrow of more criticism, punishment, and humiliation.

You can learn to access your soothing system through self-compassion, so you can navigate those painful moments of doubt without emotionally hurting yourself more or feeding into the procrastination loop.

Learning to lean on your self-soothing system with self-compassion practices will help you feel more energized, alert, and motivated to get things done!

Developing self-compassion is like stopping the second arrow. It is moving you to face what scares you with courage. Being kind to yourself is a bold move.

YOUR COMPASSIONATE SELF

We all carry within us a compassionate presence that is gentle, wise and warm.

Wherever you are, this caring part of yourself comes with you. It just happens that, with the business of life, the laundry lists of things you have to do, and the way you respond to the cycle of procrastination, you sometimes forget how to access that part of yourself. (To clarify, when I say "parts of you," this is a metaphor to highlight that, biologically speaking, we're wired to be kind to each other and to ourselves.)

Paul Gilbert, the developer of Compassion Focused Therapy (CFT), states that when you use an image of your compassionate self and are "in its presence, you can be yourself; there is no need to pretend to be what you are not. It completely understands you, accepts you, and is loving toward you" (Gilbert and Choden 2014, p.243).

ACTIVITY: Visualizing your compassionate self

You can tap into the power of imagery to cultivate a caring relationship with yourself. When you imagine something, parts of your brain act as if that thing is present in reality. See for yourself.

In this exercise, I invite you to create the image of your best ally: your compassionate self. Think about that part of you that is wise, courageous and kind. Answer the following questions:

- What does your compassionate self look like? (Is it an older or younger version or yourself? What is this compassionate soul wearing? Can you see colors?)

  . . . .

  . . . .

- What facial expressions does your compassionate self have? (Ponder the eyes, mouth, forehead and overall look.)

· ·

· ·

- What do the voice and tone of your compassionate self sound like? (Is it loud, soft, tender, sweet, or something else?)

· ·

· ·

- What gestures does your compassionate self display?

· ·

· ·

Imagine you're openly sharing all the self-doubting and critical thoughts your mind comes up with when engaging in procrastinating actions with your compassionate self. Ask yourself what your compassionate self would say to you right now.

· ·

· ·

· ·

· ·

· ·

· ·

· ·

· ·

COMPASSIONATELY RESPONDING TO SELF-CRITICISM

People who treat themselves with compassion are more resilient (Marshall *et al.* 2015), more motivated to improve after a mistake (Breines and Chen 2012), better at receiving negative feedback (Leary *et al.* 2007), and have higher re-engagement with goals (Neely *et al.* 2009). Isn't self-compassion powerful?

In the next exercise, I wholeheartedly invite you to spend a few minutes making room to approach your harsh self-criticisms with a supportive and warm response.

ACTIVITY: Meeting my critical self with kindness

Find a place where you can sit or stand comfortably for ten minutes. Bring your awareness to your breathing with every exhale and inhale.

After a couple of moments, visualize in your mind one of those moments in which you intentionally chose to put things off, either when thinking about starting the activity or in the middle of it. Can you visualize your critical self? What does your critical self tell you?

....

....

....

....

....

Hold on to this image for a moment. Make sure you can see how this critical self looks, sounds, and feels. Greet your critical self, acknowledge it, and name it. Notice how your body feels and the emotions coming your way.

Label those sensations and emotions for what they are. Say to yourself, "I'm noticing this (sensation) in my body; I'm noticing this (feeling)."

Next, imagine your compassionate self is next to you; do your best to bring into your mind this compassionate self as it looks, sounds, and feels. Imagine this wise, courageous, and compassionate self fully gets what you're going through in this particular moment.

This compassionate self also understands that we all have tricky brains that we did not choose for ourselves; this compassionate self understands that your brain is responding as it usually does when it feels scared, anxious, or worried. This compassionate self is grounded and able to hang in there with stressful feelings.

Now, holding on to the image of your compassionate self and your willingness to be caring and supportive, how would your compassionate self communicate with you when your critical self shouts at you?

. . . .

. . . .

. . . .

. . . .

. . . .

What would your compassionate self tell your inner critic? Is there a way your compassionate self could alleviate, in a caring way, the inner critic that is showing up in this moment?

. . . .

. . . .

. . . .

. . . .

. . . .

Do your best to imagine your compassionate self's tone of voice, their gestures, the sounds of their words, and notice how it feels to be the recipient of gentleness at this moment.

What was this exercise like for you?

Using self-compassion skills in the moment, you can stop beating yourself up, dwelling on mistakes, and relentless self-criticism.

You may wonder at times, if my critical self doesn't help me to pursue my values and adds guilt, shame, and hurt in my life, what's the purpose of it?

My response to you is in the next section.

UNDERSTANDING YOUR CRITICAL SELF

Your mind, like a nagging neighbor or badgering relative, has learned to protect you in a very obnoxious way: attacking you with more self-criticism so you don't make a fool of yourself, do something you're not equipped for, or that could expose your faults. That's why many researchers think of self-criticism as a safety behavior (Kim 2005; Salkovskis 1996; Thwaites and Freeston 2005).

Gilbert and Choden (2014) identified two main functions of self-criticism: self-correction or improvement, and persecution or punishment. One function is punitive, harmful, and focuses on beating you up and making you feel small, not because you carry an enemy within you but because your mind has learned to deal with pain and protect you in a harsh way.

The other function, compassionate self-correction, focuses on learning from a painful situation and the steps you need to take to grow, flourish, and move forward in life.

When your critical self shows up, you have a choice. You can either continue with the punitive, harsh voice or you can tap into compassionate self-correction by taking a deep breath, staying present, and acknowledging that there is something that your critical self is trying to protect you from in that specific moment.

You can ask yourself: What is your critical self protecting you from in a very annoying way? What are you afraid will happen if your critical self is not there screaming at you?

ACTIVITY: What's the most prominent function of your critical self?

How does your critical self impact your life? Does it motivate you to interrupt the procrastination loop or does it discourage you from doing so?

. . . .

. . . .

. . . .

. . . .

. . . .

In the next activity, you will dive deeper into compassionate self-correction.

ACTIVITY: Compassionate self-correction

For this activity, recall a moment in which you were trapped in a cycle of procrastination and your criticizing self was right there, next to you, running the show. Jot down the situation below.

. . . .

. . . .

. . . .

. . . .

. . . .

Answer these questions:

What personal value is your critical self inviting you to keep present in a bothersome way in this moment?

. . . .

. . . .

. . . .

. . . .

. . . .

What is your critical self asking you to pay attention to in this annoying way? Is there any internal experience or external factor for you to consider in this moment?

. . . .

. . . .

. . . .

. . . .

. . . .

Bring into your mind your compassionate self, and ask yourself, what does your compassionate self encourage you to do with your feet, hands, and mouth? What action can you take at this moment that is consistent with your values?

....

....

....

....

....

From now on, rather than running away from those self-criticizing thoughts, challenging them, pretending they don't exist, or attacking yourself, I encourage you to compassionately respond to them.

WRAPPING UP

Do you remember the Buddhist parable from the beginning of the chapter?

In this chapter, you have tackled your first arrow—the two core psychological processes—that push you to procrastinate about your life and the stuff you need to get done: self-criticism and self-doubt.

By actively pursuing caring responses when needed, practicing self-compassion with openness, tapping into compassionate self-correction, and holding on to your values as your life-compass, you can free yourself from suffering from procrastination and move toward a joyful life.

You got this!

CHAPTER 5

COMPASSIONATE ACCOUNTABILITY

You have learned about the core psychological processes that drive and maintain procrastinating habits, and the intersection between procrastination and other struggles. In Chapters 3 and 4, you explored your heart's deepest desires for how you want to live your life and how to deal with the tricky thoughts, "It's too late" and "What's the point?" when pursuing your values.

Being human is very challenging and, instead of going along with your critical self, I truly hope you are cultivating a compassionate mind and practicing compassionate responses as you learned in Chapter 4.

To continue understanding and tackling the causes of procrastinating habits, think briefly of one of your earliest memories of procrastination.

Perhaps you didn't pay a parking ticket because it was due a long time in the future, but in the end, the amount you owed accumulated interest. Maybe you kept postponing a doctor's appointment because you felt anxious every time you thought about contacting the doctor's office. Or maybe you stopped attending a class because you missed a paper and felt embarrassed about it.

It wasn't your intention to procrastinate. It wasn't your intention for each one of those situations to grow into a pattern of procrastination habits. You didn't plan for the pattern of procrastination to spread into other areas of your life. You didn't commit to doing something with the intention of dropping the ball later.

In each one of these procrastination events, you—like every person I work with—did exactly what your mind told you to do. The truth is that it's complicated and exhausting to have a demanding mind that pushes you to act in the blink of an eye without carefully looking at the choices in front of you. It's hard to quickly take action on your thoughts.

To break the habit of postponing things and quickly going along with your pushy mind, you need to deal with two types of thoughts that drive you to leave projects high and dry: reasons and rules.

COZY REASONS AND RIGID RULES

Let's start this section with an activity. Please read the directions for the activity below, put this workbook down, and pause reading it for one week. (Yup, you read that correctly!)

ACTIVITY: Paying attention to your thinking, for real!

For the next seven days, every time you're considering starting an activity you've been wrestling with or you're in the middle of it and have the urge to stop working on it, write down all those thoughts that show up in your mind using the prompts below.

You don't need to do anything else with those thoughts besides observing them, watching them, and writing them down as they happen. No need to go into editing mode! The more you capture the words or images, the better!

Day of the week

. . . .

What's the activity you wanted to take care of?

. . . .

What thoughts showed up?

. . . .

. . . .

What did you do?

. . . .

. . . .

. . . .

. . . .

What did you notice when paying attention to your thinking? Are there any repetitive and frequent themes? Did you go along with these thoughts and do what they asked you to do?

It's quite likely that, when approaching a project or when you're in the middle of it, this is the inner chat that goes on in your mind:

You: I need to find a new accountant for my office.

Your mind's response:

- I'm too tired right now.
- I don't feel it within me to do it.
- It's exhausting having to chat on the phone and interview people.
- It won't take too long; I have time.

- I don't have enough time right now; better to do this when I have a larger chunk of time.
- It's not very important; I can stay with my old accountant for another year.
- There are so many documents to go over; it's too much right now.
- I'll feel so annoyed looking at personal websites.
- This isn't procrastination; I really need to think more about hiring a new accountant.

Your mind's reply three minutes later:

- I need to read all their reviews first before I contact a potential accountant.
- I need to clear my schedule before I can start working on this new hire.
- I work better under pressure, so I'd better wait until next year when I really need a new accountant.
- I can't hire an accountant before organizing my accounting files.
- I don't feel motivated to go through the hassle of hiring a new accountant right now.
- The setting doesn't feel right for taking care of things.
- I don't feel the enthusiasm or strong desire I need to start this hiring process.

It's like your mind almost immediately comes up with these thoughts, variations of them or similar ones each time you're about to take on a new task.

Your mind thinks of (1) very good reasons or explanations for why you should avoid what you need to be doing, and (2) specific requirements you must complete or take care of before handling things.

The first type of thought is called "reasons or reason-giving thoughts," and the second type is known as "rules or ruling thoughts."

Reason-giving thoughts often tell you why changing procrastination habits, checking items off your to-do- list, or doing something toward your values when facing a challenge is impractical, impossible, or unnecessary.

Ruling thoughts are like unbreakable requirements, guidelines, or orders you must follow. These rules tell you, "you must do x before doing y."

From time to time, your mind will forecast a negative outcome (e.g., this will suck) or a positive one (e.g., I'll feel better tomorrow so I'll start or complete this project then). Occasionally, your mind will make calculations about the time an activity requires as if it were the oracle of truth, without carefully looking at what's doable and what's not in the limited amount of time, energy, and resources you have every day.

Many researchers and clinicians have identified different types of reasons and rules: planning fallacy, anticipating catastrophic endings, underestimating your ability to cope, fortune telling, and trivializing thoughts. In this workbook, I'm referring to all of these as "reasons or rules," so you don't have to worry about those other categorical names and can focus more on catching them as they happen and how they "work" in your life.

The bottom line is that your mind is excellent at coming up with reasons and rules for why you can't approach an activity that is important to you, or why you shouldn't get better at managing procrastination.

ACTIVITY: Going back to check your thinking!

Go back to the log from the last activity, "Paying attention to your thinking, for real!" Make a circle around all the ruling thoughts and a rectangle around the reason-giving thoughts you get trapped by.

What do you notice when observing your thinking with your open eyes, as if you are observing a painting? Which one of these thoughts—rules or reasons—does your mind bring to the forefront most for you?

. . . .

. . . .

. . . .

. . . .

. . . .

. . . .

. . . .

Of course, there is a kernel of truth in all these rules and reasons. Sometimes you will feel too tired to do a task or won't have the time you need to take care of something, and that's understandable.

You may need to have in your hands important documents before completing a task. Having ruling thoughts and reason-giving thoughts in your mind is not the problem. The challenge is recognizing how often or quickly you let them command your actions.

I'm not saying that if you feel tired you should stay awake all night, ignore your body, or pretend you're fresh. I'm also not saying you should be reckless and unprepared when interviewing a job candidate. But I am saying that, before following these thoughts to a T, you should check whether you're responding to them habitually or are making an intentional choice about how to behave.

Let's take a quick detour for a minute. Have you ever experienced a painful breakup that was really hard to face? When someone asked you what happened, without planning your response, your mind quickly responded, "She did this…, she did that…, she said this…, she said that…" and so on. At that moment, your mind was making sense of the sorrow of the breakup by coming up with reasons and explanations about the other person's behaviors and what happened because slowing down and saying what you were feeling, sharing the regrets you had, or making room for the sadness that comes with a rupture was too much to go through.

Your mind does the same.

Your mind tells you that stuff outside of you has happened and that's why you're postponing it (e.g., they didn't call me; they didn't email me; no one told me exactly what I needed to do or when I needed to get it done by). Other times, your mind focuses on your internal resources or experiences as the sources of your procrastinating habits (e.g., I don't feel like; I don't have time; it's not important).

Ayayay with our minds!

You're not alone. At this precise moment, hundreds of people are dealing with the same push and pull over whether to get things done or to procrastinate, to face or to avoid discomfort, and to take steps toward their values or away from them.

Your mind has learned to solve this push-and-pull dilemma by relying on all types of narratives, reasons, and rules, confusing them with facts and demanding you act based on them.

On top of that, and here is the tricky part, all that thinking sounds rational and reasonable in those moments, but when taken as the absolute truth, all those thoughts point you in one direction only: to stop doing what you're doing, ignore your values, and forget the long-term consequences of your choices.

It's not your fault. Your mind is doing, and will continue to do, what everyone's mind does when facing pain or anticipating any type of distress: trying to solve it right away by coming up with stuff in your head. *Some of the stuff is helpful, but a lot of the stuff your mind thinks is not helpful.*

It's like your mind is a glitchy helper trying to run the show, only focusing on avoiding anything that makes you feel uncomfortable. And, of course, this glitchy helper of yours gets super-active when approaching what's important to you. It's like the more you care, the busier your mind gets.

You can make a shift in your life and break procrastination habits by approaching those cozy thoughts and rigid rules with…

COMPASSIONATE ACCOUNTABILITY

The word compassion comes from two Latin words: *com,* which means together, and *pati,* which means to suffer. Being compassionate means making room for our difficulties, struggles, and sorrows as they happen.

It means opening up to your internal discomfort as it comes, without judging it or judging yourself for being in discomfort, comparing it to other people's difficulties, blaming yourself for starting it, or listing reasons why you shouldn't be having a hard time. Compassion is recognizing that you're experiencing hardship in a given moment and doing something about it.

Dealing with a procrastination pattern is painful because it costs you friendships, career opportunities, social gatherings, your health, and more. It's also difficult because your mind doesn't know other ways to manage those convincing reasons, tricky rules, and painful narratives when encountering a project. That's why you need compassionate skills.

In Chapter 4, Be Good to Yourself!, you visualized your compassionate self in response to your critical self. In this chapter, I want to invite you to take your compassionate skills one step further by practicing compassionate accountability.

When you read the words "compassionate accountability," what do you think of?

· ·

· ·

· ·

· ·

· ·

· ·

I think of compassionate accountability as the act of genuinely accepting that your struggle to take care of things is real, is not going away, and that you're willing to do what's within your control to manage it skillfully and toward becoming the person you want to be.

Being compassionately accountable is like being unconditionally there for yourself when your mind quickly thinks of reasons, rules, or criticisms that pull you to abandon a project.

When you're compassionately accountable, you acknowledge you're struggling to get things done and take 100 percent responsibility for your actions, no matter what your mind tells you.

In the next pages, you'll learn skills to be compassionately accountable and manage those problematic delaying strategies as they happen.

NOTICING AND NAMING

Before responding to or acting on the rules, reasons, and other stuff your mind comes up with, *you need to start noticing and naming them.*

"Don't be ridiculous," my friend told me when we were chatting about this skill. "I already know what I'm thinking when procrastinating, so I'm already there with my thoughts," he added.

To many people, watching your thoughts, labeling them, and making room for them sounds like a very simplistic thing to do, or even ridiculous.

What kind of therapist or coach would suggest something like that?

Here's the deal: Being able to watch, label, and make room for all those reasons and ruling thoughts in your mind will help you react less automatically to them and do more of the stuff you need to do.

Noticing and naming is an intentional action to give yourself space to respond to those noisy thoughts and check which actions take you toward or away from what you care about. It's like you're taking a pause before getting caught up in your thinking and reactively jumping into action.

For a moment, go back to your experience with procrastinating behaviors: How have your career, health, or friendships been impacted when you've quickly done what those reasoning and rigid rules suggest you do? Did you do more or less in those areas of your life?

If you've read this far, it's because you know, deep inside, that continuing to rely on those familiar thoughts and being bossed around by them has negatively affected your relationships, work performance, well-being, or finances.

I encourage you to have an open attitude as you learn and practice the skills of noticing and naming. Let's be clear that when you're noticing and naming all those rules and reasons, the goal is not to have less of them but to get better at having them, while choosing what to do in the service of your values in the long run.

ACTIVITY: Noticing the noise in your head

This activity has three parts; you need a timer for all of them. There is no right or wrong way of doing these exercises; you're noticing your internal experiences for what they are.

Part 1

Set the timer for two minutes, close this book, and watch the thoughts that show up in your mind. By thoughts, I'm referring to images, thoughts about this exercise, dreams, questions, your to-do list, feeling words, and so on. Think of thoughts as all the mental activity that goes on in your mind all the time. When the timer goes off, open this page and complete the exercise below.

I noticed these thoughts...

....

....

....

....

....

I noticed these feelings...

....

....

....

....

....

I noticed these sensations...

....

....

....

....

....

Part 2

Set the timer for five minutes, close this book, and watch the thoughts that show up in your mind and the feelings or sensations that come along. When the timer goes off, open this page and complete the exercise below.

I had these thoughts...

....

....

....

....

....

I had these feelings...

....

....

....

....

....

I had these sensations...

....

....

....

....

....

Part 3

Set the timer for ten minutes, close this book, and watch the thoughts that show up in your mind and the feelings or sensations that come along. When the timer goes off, open this page and complete the exercise below.

I watched these thoughts...

. . . .

. . . .

. . . .

. . . .

. . . .

I watched these feelings...

. . . .

. . . .

. . . .

. . . .

. . . .

I watched these sensations...

. . . .

. . . .

. . . .

. . . .

. . . .

Let's take this activity a step further.

ACTIVITY: Noticing and labeling your inner experiences

Read the script below and record it using a device of your choice. Then listen to the recording in a quiet space as you gently focus your eyes on a single point.

Get in a comfortable place where you won't be disturbed. Start by taking a few deep breaths. Allow yourself to settle into the moment and slowly start bringing your attention to your thinking.

Pay close attention to each thought your mind creates.

Notice if a single thought seems to arise or if thoughts come and go. Watch your thoughts.

Be aware of each thought as it comes into your mind as much as possible. As soon as you become aware of a fully formed thought, make a mental note of it and say "thought."

Don't try to analyze or hold on to the thought.

Don't believe or disbelieve the thoughts.

Just acknowledge all the thoughts showing up in your mind.

Keep noticing. When you notice a thought, whisper the word "thinking" softly in your mind.

If you find you are judging yourself for having a thought, just notice that. Don't argue with your mind's judgment.

Just notice it for what it is and label it as thinking. There is thinking.

The key to this exercise is to notice all the thoughts that show up in your mind. Rather than analyzing them, arguing against them, or holding on to them, just notice them.

Keep breathing. Keep watching.

Keep whispering the word "thinking" softly in your mind.

Having a thought doesn't mean you have to react to the thought.

As you watch your mind, notice that some thoughts are quick fragments. Other thoughts are loud and fully formed. Other thoughts are images. Notice them and name them as "thinking."

There's no need to analyze any of those thoughts or hold on to them. There's no need to believe or disbelieve. Just acknowledge the thinking.

Now, slowly switch your attention to the sensations in your body and the feelings that come with it. Gently label these as "feeling or sensing." Don't worry about finding the perfect name for the feeling or the perfect name for the sensations; just notice them and label them "feeling or sensing."

Continue breathing and focusing on that sensation or feeling. Watch the sensation or feeling moving in your body or staying in a particular location; just watch it, and as you do so, label it "feeling" or "sensing."

Every feeling and sensation may ask you to do something, to pay attention to something else, to distract… Or these feelings or sensations may prompt you to avoid something. Keep watching them gently as they happen. Watch their intensity: are they loud or soft? Notice their location. Gently label them "sensing" or "feeling."

Keep breathing. Keep noticing the feeling or the sensation.

Keep whispering the words "feeling" or "sensing" softly in your mind as you label your inner experiences.

If an image pops up or your mind wanders, as our minds do, label that as "thinking."

As you continue this exercise, do your best to label all these inner experiences as they happen. Label thoughts or images or worries or any random mental construction that shows up in your mind as "thinking." Continue to label the reactions in your body as "sensing" and the feelings that call your attention as "feeling."

If you find yourself interacting with your thoughts, or dwelling on your feelings or sensations, or resisting and fighting back with more thinking, or quickly trying to distract yourself, notice those reactions and bring yourself back to observing the thinking, feeling, and sensing as it happens.

You don't need to do anything besides watch, observe, and make room for the internal experiences.

Watch the flow of all the stuff that happens inside you.

Not every internal experience requires you to act or react.

Thinking is thinking.

Feeling is feeling.

Sensing is sensing.

Keep labeling your internal experiences as they happen.

Keep labeling thinking, feeling, and sensing as they happen.

Remember, you are a person having, watching, and noticing experiences. You are not the experiences themselves. You're more like a container for those experiences.

Take a deep breath as you finish this exercise of noticing and labeling your inner experiences.

You have finished practicing the skill of noticing, observing, and watching your thoughts; in this last exercise, you also noticed and labelled your feelings and sensations.

Let's move these micro-skills one notch up so you can continue tackling those psychological barriers that feed into procrastination.

ACTIVITY: Noticing and naming your cozy rules and rigid reasons

Choose one area of your life that you want to focus on for this exercise.

. . . .

. . . .

. . . .

What's the activity you have been putting off in this area of your life?

. . . .

. . . .

· ·

· ·

· ·

What are the rules and reasons your mind just came up with that led you to procrastinate this activity?

· ·

· ·

· ·

· ·

· ·

Moving forward, how would you name these reasons and rules? You can choose any name that works for you!

· ·

· ·

· ·

Read the directions below before completing this part of the exercise. Imagine for a moment that you're taking care of this activity with as much detail as possible, so you can see it as if you're watching a movie.

Stay with this image for a couple of moments. Watch your mind. Check what your mind, your unconditional helper, does. If your mind screams a ruling thought at you, using your inside voice, say the name you choose for it: "Here is [enter the name]" or label it as "rule." If you notice a reason-giving thought, do the same. If your critical self shows up, name it as you did in

Chapter 4, Be Good to Yourself! You can always say, "Hello, my old friend, Mr. Criticism!"

Stay with the visualization for at least two to three minutes.

You can use these skills together—noticing and naming—every time you want to complete a project and your glitchy helper makes a noise. You're practicing the skill of "having thoughts without reacting quickly to them." The more you intentionally make room for the stuff that your mind generates, the more you can choose your actions.

Your mind also needs to...

WATCH OUT FOR MINIMIZING THOUGHTS!

Mohammed, a graduate student of theology, was passionate about his studies. At the beginning of his studies, he was often ready to participate in class debates, volunteer for extracurricular activities and talk about the subjects he was studying with anyone that asked him how school was going.

When asked to write an essay, he loved to dive deeply into it, and, as a result, he would write comprehensive and long-format essays instead of the short essays most of his classmates submitted.

As the academic demands increased for Mohammed, despite how much he cared for his studies, he only submitted two complete papers during the semester. He couldn't finish the others because he felt they weren't good enough.

Mohammed felt overwhelmed by all the research articles he needed to read. He told himself he would read them on the day of the deadline; on the day of the deadline, he ended up skipping class because he felt ashamed about not finishing his reading.

When Mohammed saw his three F grades, he felt like hiding from his classmates so no one would learn about them.

He got upset with himself, asking "What's wrong with me? I'm just a lazy bum." Then he looked at his grades again and thought, "It would have been worse if I'd got four or five Fs; at least I only got three Fs. I guess three Fs is better than six Fs." He grabbed his pencil and started drawing, then went back to texting his boyfriend.

When things go wrong—for example, you get a late fee for a parking ticket, run out of groceries, lose a client, become unreliable with your friends—due to procrastinating actions, your mind tells you, "It wasn't that bad; it could have been worse."

Those thoughts have a purpose: distracting you from taking ownership of your actions and minimizing the embarrassment of having put something off. I call those thoughts "minimizing thoughts."

Your mind, as usual, is doing what it knows to do: putting all resources into protecting you from feeling bad about or disappointed in yourself. Your mind is saying, "Don't go there, that feels bad and yucky. Better cheer yourself up; focus on the positive."

Unfortunately, you cannot build a life you love and break those procrastinating habits by brushing off the consequences of your choices.

I know it's difficult to make room for the embarrassment, guilt, and distress that comes when looking at the outcome of your actions. That's why self-forgiveness and being compassionately accountable are important (if you want to revisit self-forgiveness skills, see Chapter 3, Finding the Compass of Your Life).

This is why being compassionately accountable is important: because you need to recognize the inherent difficulties of having a mind that is creative at coming up with minimizing thoughts and take ownership of the choices you make in those moments.

This doesn't mean you have to spend hours attacking yourself for the choices you make. But it does mean that when your mind brings all types of thinking noise, you take 100 percent responsibility for your actions, and intentionally slow down to check what you truly care about in those circumstances.

When your mind thinks a minimizing thought, gently ask yourself:

- What is my mind trying to protect me from with these minimizing thoughts right now?
- What can I learn from this situation to be who I want to be in the future?
- Instead of going along with my minimizing thoughts and brushing things off, what am I willing to do differently next time to create a life worth living in the long run?

Asking yourself those questions will allow you to choose your behaviors, instead of being a puppet of those minimizing thoughts.

As you take care of things and slow down to catch the different types of noise your mind brings to the forefront, you may begin to notice distressing feelings demanding your attention. This is natural.

We'll dive into how to handle another key psychological process of procrastination: those daunting emotions that tend to arise when you're focusing on what matters most. By learning how to skillfully and compassionately approach those feelings, you will find it easier to complete tasks and move forward with your day.

PESKY FEELINGS

Let's think about Sarah for a moment.

Sarah is a junior editor, working for a local publishing company and passionate about written communication. She has a very sophisticated vocabulary, is enthusiastic for narrating short stories, and loves editing of all types, from editing the grammar and structure of each sentence in a document to developmental editing and everything in between.

While Sarah is qualified for her current role and has previous experience in similar roles, she has been having a hard time replying to emails and internal messages from her coworkers and managers in this new job.

In her attempts to manage this delay in her communication, Sarah blocked half an hour into her schedule, three times a day, to focus only on responding to anyone waiting for her. "In this way, I won't be interrupted when working on manuscripts," she thought.

This is what Sarah experienced in that half hour:

- "It's noon, time to check my email."
- Sarah briefly scans the sender and subjects of the emails:
  - Subject: Donna's manuscript deadline is March 14th
  - Subject: Waiting for a reply; did you receive this email?
  - Subject: Checking on your part for Tim's book
  - Subject: Need to schedule a one-on-one meeting; are you there?
  - Subject: New acquisitions meeting Wednesday 9–11 a.m.
  - Subject: Did you book your ticket?

Sarah continues reading the subjects of the emails.

- Her heartbeat speeds up and she feels a familiar shortness of breath.
- A wave of heat goes through her body. Sarah passes her right hand over her forehead; next, she adjusts her posture in her chair and opens randomly one email.
- "I can't do this. I won't make it on time for the meeting. Augghhhh. I guess I can show up to the meeting on Friday. I'll have enough time to put together a report, it should be fine."

- "Which manuscript should I work on this afternoon? This sucks." She swallows slowly.
- Sarah feels the sweatiness slowly building in her hands.
- "I don't feel like replying to each email right now; it's too much. I need to read everything they have sent me before replying," Sarah thinks, rubbing her sweaty hands together.
- Sarah imagines her manager's office, the bright painting on the wall behind her desk, the pile of documents on the left side of the desk, and the yellow, turquoise, pink, and blue highlighters spread out on it. Next, she quickly imagines her manager handing her the quarterly evaluation and reading on the first page, in capital and bold letters, "Doesn't meet expectations and needs a remediation plan."
- Sarah stares at the screen as if she's reading an email. She sees the printed letters, but, with every letter, her breath becomes shorter and a pressure in her chest starts.
- Sarah quickly opens a new browser window and starts searching for a bathing suit for her next beach vacation, sighing. She briefly looks around the office, looks down, and feels embarrassed about having a hard time replying to emails.

Have you been in Sarah's shoes?

As we're thinking beings, we're also feeling beings.

Sarah is a competent professional, but when managing her inbox—an everyday task for her—she immediately feels a visceral rush of overwhelming feelings and ends up making short-term decisions and chasing good feelings.

ACTIVITY: What feelings have you gotten stuck with this week?

Think about the last time you struggled with an unpleasant task. Briefly describe it and jot down the feelings that came along with it. Don't worry about providing a perfect description of this feeling or identifying it exactly.

....

....

....

....

....

....

....

....

....

....

....

....

Borkovec and colleagues (1998) discovered that people struggling with chronic worry often get caught up in endless "what-if" scenarios, using these imagined futures as a way to sidestep the intense emotions that accompany anxiety. Their research revealed that chronic worriers struggled to identify their own feelings, believed that uncomfortable emotions will last forever and assumed that others around them didn't struggle with emotions as much as they do.

As an anxious procrastinator, you may relate to this research findings.

ACTIVITY: What are the emotions you get stuck on in general?

Look at the following list of emotions, and check the ones you experience when feeling the urge to put things off. Feel free to add any other emotion words that capture how you're feeling at the end of the list.

Anxious	Guilty	Unsure
Ashamed	Helpless	Upset
Confused	Hopeless	Useless
Defeated	Lonely	Worried
Dejected	Mad	Worthless
Disconnected	Motivated	. . . .
Disgusted	Overwhelmed	. . . .
Distracted	Powerless	. . . .
Doubtful	Preoccupied	. . . .
Embarrassed	Regretful	. . . .
Excited	Sad	. . . .
Enthusiastic	Tearful	. . . .
Fearful	Tired	. . . .
Frustrated	Uneasy	. . . .

As you unpack the emotional experience of a procrastination episode, it's helpful to also notice what happens in your body. There is no feeling without a bodily sensation and, at times, you may be more attuned to those physical sensations than anything else.

ACTIVITY: Noticing pesky sensations

To notice the uncomfortable sensations you get stuck with, circle the words describing physical sensations you might experience when having those feelings.

Agitated	Heavy	Tight
Anxious	Jagged	Tired
Breathless	Jittery	Unsettled
Chilled	Jumpy	Weary
Choked up	Nauseous/sick	Worked up
Churned up	Numb	. . . .
Clenched	On edge	. . . .
Cramped	Pounding	. . . .
Deflated	Pressure	. . . .
Drained	Restless	. . . .
Dull	Shaky	. . . .
Empty	Suffocated	. . . .
Exhausted	Sweaty	. . . .
Flat	Tense	. . . .
Frozen	Tender	. . . .

Emotions, including the uncomfortable ones, provide you with information to make decisions, data about a situation, motivate you to leap into action, and help you to communicate effectively with others about your likes, dislikes, needs, and wants. Every emotion pushes you to do something! That's the gift and the curse of being an emotional being.

If you're a super-feeler—a person who feels too much, too quickly, and acts too soon—and want to learn more skills to regulate your responses to your emotions, check out my book, *Escaping the Emotional Roller Coaster* (2018), and return to the section on emotional regulation and procrastination in Chapter 2.

As you notice and name your thoughts, you can do the same with your feelings.

ACTIVITY: Noticing and labeling your feelings

Read these directions before completing this exercise and give yourself five minutes for it.

You can stand up, sit down, or lie down, whatever feels more comfortable for you. Gently, without rushing, bring your attention to your body. Notice your body posture, the position of your arms and legs, your back, your neck, and your facial expression.

Next, imagine a moment of stuckness with a procrastinating habit. What were you hoping to accomplish? What did you end up doing? Hold on to this image as vividly as possible.

Then, notice any physical sensations that show up in your body; see if you can describe them without judging them. You can say "tension" when noticing tension or "heart beating fast" if that's happening. Just do your best to describe those sensations as they're happening.

Slowly, bring your attention to your breath. As you breathe out, ask yourself, "What emotion am I feeling right now?" Without judging yourself or the emotion you're feeling, notice it and name it for what it is.

Don't worry about having the correct name for the emotion, just notice it and name it. You can say, "I'm feeling... (name of the feeling)."

Do your best to adopt an attitude of curiosity toward your feelings, as if you're noticing them for the first time. Notice how a feeling feels in your body; notice its intensity; notice where it shows up in your body; notice whether this feeling shifts on to another feeling or if the sensations change in your body.

If your mind cooks up any thoughts or images, label them by saying, "thinking," and go back to noticing the feeling in your body. Ask yourself again, "What am I feeling right now?" Notice and name those feelings as they come and go.

What did you notice during this brief exercise?

. . . .

. . . .

. . . .

. . . .

. . . .

. . . .

To stop being pushed around by your feelings, unlearn procrastinating habits, do things consistently, and be who you want to be, you need to start noticing and naming the feelings that show up as you tackle things.

When I introduced this new skill, one client told me, "That sounds like misery." Another said that naming feelings sounded like giving up on them. "Why would I want to stay with something so uncomfortable?" they asked.

I'm not saying you need to like those feelings. Noticing and naming feelings doesn't mean you have to like them, that you should pretend they don't exist, or that you must power through them. You feel what you feel, when you feel it, and in the way you feel it.

Noticing and naming are skills you need to practice over and over to develop the ability to have a feeling, make room for a feeling, and feel a feeling, so you can choose your actions according to your *values* and not according to your *feelings*.

When you're willing to feel your feelings, let go of trying to control them, or act on them quickly, you nourish your capacity to choose and gain control of your behaviors.

ACTIVITY: Paying attention to your emotions

Every day of this week, pay attention to all aspects of your emotions. At the end of each day, reflect on one difficult feeling you experienced and answer the following prompts.

What's the emotion you want to focus on?

....

What was going on when you felt this emotion (what was the situation)?

....

....

....

....

....

What was important to you in that situation? What was your personal value?

....

....

....

....

....

What did you notice in your body?

· ·

· ·

· ·

· ·

· ·

What did you feel like doing based on this emotion?

· ·

· ·

· ·

· ·

· ·

What did you do?

· ·

· ·

· ·

· ·

· ·

Sometimes, acting on your emotions will take you closer to your values and sometimes it will not (I'll explain this further later in this chapter).

BUT, WHAT IF IT'S ALL TOO OVERWHELMING?

Dealing with overwhelming feelings seems like the hardest thing to do, but intentionally taking an open, accepting, and gentle attitude toward them will give you the freedom to do more of the stuff you want to do.

Think of dealing with overwhelming feelings as if you are in quicksand full of emotions. What would you do if you were in quicksand? You'd feel pressured, stuck, and physically uncomfortable because quicksand is denser than the human body. Most people would start moving quickly and swim abruptly. But the more you fight against the density of the quicksand, the more the emotions will suck you under.

To skillfully manage this quicksand of distressing emotions, you need to do something that feels very counterintuitive in the moment. You need to stop fighting against the upsetting feelings by dwelling on them, criticizing them, or judging them. Instead, intentionally imagine leaning back as you're lying down on the quicksand and let the feelings be.

Imagine you're making small, gentle back-and-forth motions with your legs, so the sand, or the feelings, around you loosen up and you can float better.

The more you purposefully lie on your back and let the feelings naturally unfold, the more you are in charge of your actions and the harder it will be to sink beneath those emotions.

By letting the overwhelming emotions be, you can manage them and the stress of the moment without making it worse for yourself.

ACTIVITY: Compassionately responding to an overwhelming feeling

Read the directions below while recording your voice in any recording device you want to use. Then, listen to the recording and follow the directions.

Find a comfortable seated position, with your feet flat on the floor and your hands resting gently on your thighs. You can also lie down or stand up if that's better for you. Just place your body in a relaxed position.

Close your eyes if you feel good doing so, or focus your gaze on a single point in the room. Gently and without rushing, take a few slow, deep breaths in through your nose, filling your lungs completely, and then exhale slowly through your mouth.

See if you can slow your breathing down a little more.

Inhale deeply through your nose to the count of four. Feel your abdomen expand as you fill your lungs with air: 1, 2, 3, 4. Hold your breath for a moment before breathing out, counting to two: 1, 2. Breathe out, exhaling slowly and completely through your mouth, counting to six: 1, 2, 3, 4, 5, 6. Pause briefly for a moment: 1, 2.

Gently continue with this soothing rhythm a couple of times.

Inhale through your nose: 1, 2, 3, 4.

Hold it: 1, 2.

Exhale through your mouth: 1, 2, 3, 4, 5, 6.

Pause for 1, 2.

Notice how it feels to intentionally breathe slowly as you practice soothing rhythmic breathing.

Now think of a difficult emotion you experience when needing to take care of things. Hold the situation that triggered this feeling in your mind, noticing all the details of it as if you're watching a movie. Notice how it feels in this moment, holding on to that event, without rushing, simply noticing. Check the sensations in your body and softly describe them as they are; check the action that this emotion pushes you toward. What do you feel like doing? Focus on this sensation and feeling in your body and watch it as if you're watching a scene from a movie. Does it move? How big is it? Does it have a color? Watch the thoughts showing up in your mind as they happen. What's your inner dialogue telling you?

Keep watching this feeling as if you're watching different scenes from a movie. If you're feeling overwhelmed by this emotion, press your feet hard against the floor, wiggle your toes, and reconnect with your breathing. Practice your soothing rhythmic breathing for a couple of moments.

Inhale through your nose: 1, 2, 3, 4.

Hold it: 1, 2.

Exhale through your mouth: 1, 2, 3, 4, 5, 6.

Pause for 1, 2.

When you're ready, go back and hold on to this triggering event and watch the emotion that emerges again. Watch the sensations, the urges, and the thoughts that arise, without doing anything but watching them. Allow yourself to be fully present with this distressing feeling.

Bring into mind your compassionate self, the resilient and wise part of you that unconditionally supports you, loves you, and cares for you. What would your compassionate self do, or suggest you do? How would your compassionate self encourage you to ground yourself as this emotion comes and goes?

Can you see the facial expressions or gestures of your compassionate self toward you? What would your compassionate self tell you to remind you that big emotions come and go and that you need to fight them?

Can you receive all the caring your compassionate self offers without resisting it, and without judging yourself? Make room for the understanding and encouragement of your compassionate self as you deserve it in this moment of pain.

Notice how it feels to be the recipient of kindness when you feel swamped by a loud feeling in your body. Notice your reactions as you experience kindness. Notice what happened to that intense feeling you were focusing on in this exercise.

Observe your experience without dwelling on it. Observe your experience without attaching to how you are supposed to feel or whether this exercise worked or not. Observe your experience with curious eyes and openness.

Gently, take a few slow breaths as you finish this exercise.

Make some notes about your experience below.

. . . .

. . . .

. . . .

. . . .

. . . .

. . . .

. . . .

. . . .

. . . .

. . . .

. . . .

. . . .

. . . .

. . . .

As you start making headway with your tasks and meeting your deadlines, keep in mind that the feelings that feed into the procrastinating habits will still be there. Knocking out tasks means saying, "Hello, [name of the feeling]." Notice and name those feelings.

If you encounter a very distressing feeling, draw on your compassionate self as another skill for self-regulation in those moments. Ground yourself with your soothing rhythmic breathing, as you did in the exercise above. Return to your values and choose your actions.

ILLUSIONS ABOUT THINKING, FEELING, AND SENSING

Let me ask you a few questions:

- Do you enjoy throwing a joke into a conversation but hold back to avoid hurting someone?
- Have you experienced moments in which you felt completely angry but acted calmly?
- Have you encountered times when you felt like leaving a dinner but stayed out of respect for the host?
- Have you ever felt down but done your best to be present when attending a work meeting?

What do these memories teach you? What are they showing you?

Let's do an exercise to expand on this.

ACTIVITY: Acknowledging the gap

Read the exercise below and do your best to try each item with an open attitude—really!

- Silently repeat to yourself, "I can't wiggle my toe." Say this sentence many times in your head and, as you're saying it, wiggle your toe.
- Imagine calling an ex-partner to tell them you want to get back together (but don't really call them or reach out in any way!).
- Silently say in your head, "I cannot bend my knee," as you bend your knee.
- Gently move your head to the left and then to the right as you repeat to yourself silently, "I cannot move my head."
- Think about eating all your favorite snacks at home right now without moving your feet, legs, or arms.

What did you observe when completing this exercise?

· ·

· ·

· ·

· ·

· ·

· ·

Can you imagine for a moment how it would be to act on every thought, feeling, and sensation that comes your way? How would your life look?

We're *soooooooooooo* used to believing that whatever shows up in our mind, our feelings and sensations, are dictators of our actions; that they're commands to do something. Yet, all those inner experiences are the stuff that shows up under your skin, not commands of your choices, actions, and decisions.

As you notice and name all these internal experiences—rules, reasons, minimizing thoughts, feelings, sensations, critical self—you are growing your ability to experience them without being consumed by them, or by following with procrastinating actions.

By now you may be thinking, "What do I do after I've noticed and named my internal experiences?"

Here is my response: Do what works!

WORKABILITY, WITH ACT LENSES

ACT is all about guiding you to live a rich life by being compassionately accountable and aligning with your values in any possible way you can, in your everyday life.

Doing what works—or "workability" as we say in ACT—is about checking whether your actions are a move toward the life you want to build or not. If a behavior moves you closer to your values in the long run, it's workable. If a behavior moves you further away from what matters to you, then it's not workable.

Instead of looking at behaviors as good or bad, right or wrong, or true or false, ACT encourages you to understand your actions in the context of a specific situation and in regard to your values. For example, imagine you had an exhausting day, your body signals that you need to relax, and you decide to watch Netflix to unwind; in this instance, choosing to stay at home, rest, and watch TV is workable because it aligns with your value of taking care of your well-being. However, if binge-watching becomes a way to avoid having difficult conversations, completing important tasks, or taking care of household responsibilities, then that's a different story.

Take another example: scrolling on social media after a long day might be a workable behavior if it helps you to relax and decompress; however, if it turns into hours of mindless scrolling to avoid responsibilities or uncomfortable feelings, it becomes unworkable.

WRAPPING UP

Now that you're tuned into the power of compassionate accountability, you're stepping into something truly courageous. Embracing compassionate accountability is a bold move—it's about taking ownership of your actions, even when your mind is throwing all sorts of distractions and doubts your way.

When approaching a task, and feeling pulled to listen to those cozy reasons, rules, minimizing thoughts, or acting on those feelings of overwhelm, you can start by acknowledging them—noticing and naming—and then, ask yourself, "What's a workable action I can take toward my values right now?

Noticing and naming are like your secret strengths—the skills that empower you to handle those uncomfortable thoughts, unsettling sensations and frustrating feelings while still choosing the actions that matter to you.

When practicing noticing and naming, keep in mind that the goal is not to feel less, sense less or think less; it's also not about feeling good, having positive thoughts, or chill sensations. Noticing and naming is about allowing those inner experiences to come and go—without wrestling with them in any way—and deciding how you want to behave.

It may feel strange at the beginning; however, in the long run you will suffer less because you will be living life instead of postponing it.

You don't have to listen to the glitchy helper in your mind. You're well-prepared to notice and name, choose your next values-based move, and be compassionately accountable again and again!

CHAPTER 6

ALIGNING YOUR CHOOSING WITH YOUR BEING

Many people hold the misconception that when a person suffers from procrastinating behaviors, they're not action-oriented, or they don't like the *doing* part of anything. Well, that's far from the truth!

I know that when looking at a task in front of you—whether it's going for a run, taking your car to the mechanic, or booking a concert ticket—you immediately struggle with a mind that shows up with rigid rules, crushing feelings, familiar reasons, painful self-critical thoughts, or thoughts that question the usefulness of that particular chore. All of that makes it hard for you to get started. Then, you end up making "feeling-good" choices, as I call them.

Chronic procrastination has nothing to do with not being action-oriented. It has to do with a learned pattern of avoidant behaviors.

You have learned to make feeling-good choices to protect yourself from feeling down, embarrassed, or guilty. Your instinct is to run from any triggering activity and to feel better right away; it's human. But those feeling-good choices are just another avoidant strategy that reinforces procrastination habits in the long run.

This chapter is about approaching another core psychological process that maintains a procrastination pattern: making impulsive, feeling-based, or short-term choices. It's also about humbly acknowledging the fact that you have a finite time to focus on the activities you're passionate about, the people who matter the most, and your life.

Looking back at different areas of your life over the last four weeks, what are those feeling-good choices you have made and what emotions were you avoiding?

. . . .

. . . .

. . . .

. . . .

. . . .

. . . .

. . . .

After reflecting on these prompts, it could be easy to feel frustrated with yourself for the decisions you've been making. I encourage you to pause, take a deep breath, and ask yourself: How can I offer myself a bit of kindness and understanding in this precise moment?

To live your life with less stagnation and more purpose, you need to brush up on your goal-setting skills. I mean it!

THE GOALS TRAP!

Having looked at the publications on goal setting and posts on social media, watched hundreds of YouTube videos, and read the academic literature, I can tell you that the literature on goals has gone wild—really wild.

You may be familiar with different approaches to goal setting like PACT (purposeful, actionable, continuous, trackable), NICE (near-term, input-based, controllable, energizing), STING (select one task, time yourself, ignore everything else, no breaks, give yourself a reward), SMART (specific, measurable, achievable, relevant, time-bound), or other frameworks. If so, I ask you to be patient and not to skip this section to ensure we're on the same page about how to define goals that take you closer to your values and how you want to show up in life.

Let's review the most common traps when determining your goals.

EMOTIONAL GOALS

When asking one of my coaching clients about his goals, he said, "I want to feel less anxious when working on this script."

This sounds reasonable: Who doesn't want to feel less anxious when doing something important for work? I don't think anybody has ever said, "I can't wait to feel anxious when working on this script."

Wanting to experience more or less of a particular feeling is understandable, especially when uncomfortable emotions get in the way of taking care of deadlines. The challenge is that, as you recall from Chapter 5, Compassionate Accountability, your thoughts, feelings, sensations, and all types of private experiences come and go throughout your day, non-stop.

Consider these three scenarios:

- Let's say that, as you're reading this workbook, out of the blue, an image of a trip you took to the mountains long ago bubbles into your mind. You feel nostalgic and then feel an urge to stop reading this workbook and search for photos from that trip.

- Imagine that, as you are going over your grocery list for the week (a boring task), your kitty stretches his legs, you feel tenderness toward him, and you have the urge to reach out and play with him so you don't have to think about the groceries any longer.

- Or let's say that while working on your CV, which is a pretty tedious task, the doorbell rings. You receive an envelope containing information about your taxes, feel stressed, and instead of going back to work on your CV, you grab your phone and start scrolling through Instagram.

Emotions happen within you and, naturally, you have urges to make decisions based on each of those feelings. Of course, if you experience a comfy feeling, you have urges to do more of what feels good in the moment. And if you encounter a chore that comes with uneasy feelings, naturally you may hope to "feel fewer of those feelings" when undertaking the chore.

ACTIVITY: Reflecting on emotional goals
that you got trapped by

Take a moment to think about times last week when you found yourself chasing after more positive emotions or trying to avoid uncomfortable ones. Jot down three examples where you were striving to feel more warmth or reduce unsettling feelings.

. . . .

. . . .

. . . .

. . . .

. . . .

. . . .

Setting emotion-based goals is like hoping for a magic wand that will make your uncomfortable feelings go away. But the more you focus on feeling more or less of an emotion, the more you will feel overwhelmed in the long run.

OUTCOME-BASED GOALS

You can find many recommendations about setting specific, actionable, and measurable goals. You may have even come up with goals like the following yourself:

- losing 30 pounds in three months
- getting your book on the *New York Times* best-seller list in a year
- getting a raise at work
- graduating in five years.

These goals are specific and measurable; they also describe things you want to achieve and accomplish. While they all sound good on paper, here is the caveat for all of them: they are out of your control.

Let's look at the goal of losing 30 pounds in three months. Even if you change your diet, exercise every day and hire a personal trainer, you don't know how much weight your body is going to lose every week, every month and so on.

Also, there are almost always variables outside of your control that affect outcomes. You could get sick; your landlord could ask you to move out, which disrupts your exercise and eating routines; your local gym might close.

I'm not saying you shouldn't take steps toward each one of those goals, that would be against the spirit of this workbook.

I actually hope you do take specific actions to reach each one of your goals. And also, I hope that you can see that holding tightly on to those specific outcomes is a recipe for disappointment.

Guaranteeing outcomes is outside of your control.

ACTIVITY: Recognizing the outcome goals you have been chasing

Consider the past month and identify three situations where you were focused on achieving specific outcomes that were outside your control. Jot down these moments and reflect on how they influenced your actions and mindset.

....

....

....

....

....

....

....

....

....

Having outcome goals is helpful as long as you acknowledge they're more like aspirations that can guide your actions, and you don't become overly attached to them.

Lastly, another common trap is setting mid-term goals as priorities, which is what we'll discuss next.

PRODUCTIVE PROCRASTINATION GOALS

To free yourself from procrastination, be careful not to get into the habit of setting goals for tasks that seem compelling enough to focus on but that are not the activities that will truly take you closer to building the life you want (for reference, see the section on "Productive procrastination" in Chapter 2, Breaking the Myth of the Typical Procrastinator).

For instance, I feel overwhelmed as I look at the stuff I need to take care of today: paying bills, making phone calls, running domestic errands, changing a light bulb, organizing photos on my cell phone, completing a workshop proposal, hanging pictures, reading a novel, exercising and cooking at the end of the day.

I have the strong urge to grab my cell phone and organize the photos in different folders, delete the duplicate ones, add tags to some of them, and select some for printing. I know I'll enjoy doing this chore: it will be fun, and it's something I must do at some point.

Yet, by spending time on it today, I'm reducing the time, resources, and energy I have for my other goals—exercising, writing the workshop proposal, cooking—that are time-sensitive and align my being with my doing, today and in the long run.

ACTIVITY: What productive procrastination goals have you been distracted by?

Jot down those goals that seem reasonable enough and, yet, were another form of avoiding other tasks that could expand your life in the long run in the last month.

....

....

....

....

....

....

....

....

Being aware of emotional goals, outcome-based goals, and productive pro-crastination goals is another step toward stopping reinforcing procrastina-tion habits and postponing your life.

ACT is all about inviting you to create a bold life, a life that you love, and a life that gives you a sense of purpose in every moment. Every skill you're learning in this workbook, including goal setting, goes back to your personal values and the person you want to be.

You need to start setting…

VALUES-BASED GOALS

Let's think for a moment of Serena Williams, a famous tennis player, Michael, a fictional client of mine, and a painful situation I personally encountered.

Serena Williams, an extraordinary tennis player who has won 23 Grand Slam single titles in the Australian Open, French Open, Wimbledon, and US Open, has mentioned publicly that "giving back" is one of the most important principles in her life. She supported the largest health cam-paign in Ghana, was the face for the Schools for Africa Initiative, funds centers that offer trauma-informed programs, helped the campaign Masks for Kids during the Covid-19 pandemic, mentors minority tennis players through her foundation, and invests in companies from underrepresented backgrounds—just to name a few of her philanthropic efforts.

Michael feels painfully tense and anxious when talking to strangers, acquaintances, or neighbors; he avoids making eye contact with anyone who notices him and believes that people think of him as an "awkward person." When he started his new job, he was offered the option to work remotely, which he immediately accepted so he wouldn't have to deal with the stress of facing people. However, in his heart of hearts, Michael dreams of a life filled with true connections with others and, at some point, would love to start a family. So, once a week, he makes the point of calling an old friend, just to connect, and has also assigned an hour a week to search for a therapist specializing in social anxiety and exposure therapy.

Here's something that happened to me. When I was close to finishing this book, I received a voice message from my cousin in São Paulo. "Can I talk to you?" he asked, his voice quivering. I pressed the green phone icon next to his name, Cali, on the screen of my cell phone.

"Tio Juani, meu pai [my father] is in intensive care in the hospital; they did an MRI," he said slowly, gasping.

"Do you have the medical report?" I asked.

"I just sent it to you," he replied.

"Give me a sec, I want to go over it."

As I read the two-page report, my eyes watered. No medical procedure could be done to save my Tio Juani. His death was imminent. I was able to see him and chat with him for a bit, as he was going in and out of consciousness with his pain medication; he was sometimes present, sometimes confused.

The day he passed away, I was tasked with sharing this painful news with my relatives. Every day I talked with them via video call. It was far from perfect for me to be in California while my relatives were in Bolivia, but being present with the ones I love is one of my dearest values.

Living your values is not about doing things perfectly all the time or measuring the size of your actions; it's about choosing to put your values in the driver's seat and aligning your being with your doing, even when you find yourself on a path you didn't choose.

Your values are like a compass, gently guiding you to set goals that really matter, helping you reconnect with parts of your life you've been putting off and supporting you to move in a direction that feels true and fulfilling.

Here are some examples of goals I have heard:

- I'm going to finish this chapter today.
- I'm going to contact my health insurance company today.
- I'm going to take care of the paperwork to renew my license this week.

Instead, be more specific, focus on what's under your control, and consider your values. Who, when, what, and for how long are important questions that could act as guiding principles for defining your values-based moves:

- I'm going to write for three hours on Wednesday and Friday, from 9 a.m. to 12 p.m., so I can be financially independent.
- I'm going to book one hour on Monday morning, at 10 a.m., to call my health insurance company so I can care for my body.
- I'm going to work on the renewal of my license for one hour on Tuesday at 3:30 p.m. so I can be independent.

It may feel strange at first to be so specific with your actions and link them to your values. It's like walking with new shoes: at first, they might feel a bit tight but, as you walk, they become easier to walk in.

Setting your values-based goals is a great first step. Next, you need to...

CHOOSE HOW TO SHOW UP

Before approaching a task, ask yourself: "How am I going to approach this? What qualities do I want to keep present when approaching this?"

Going back to the examples from the last section, you could approach your writing with openness to the process of writing—connecting sentences and looking at its flow—or with attachment to the idea of having the perfect writing.

You could call your health insurance company with compassion for yourself because it's stressful talking with healthcare representatives.

You could work on renewing your license by paying full attention to it instead of getting distracted by cranky thoughts or following every tangential thought your mind comes up with.

In other words, you need to choose how you approach your values-based activities. As you commit to these actions, you also need to commit to...

LEAN INTO YOUR STRUGGLE

Dr. Z.:   What did you notice as you started writing?
Client: I felt embarrassed, annoyed. It made me feel anxious. I felt like closing the laptop.

As you approach what matters, you will immediately notice that all the familiar upsetting feelings are there. That goes for every human being on earth!

Part of you wants to do something different, but another part wants to return to the old procrastination behaviors. You're not on the wrong track—you're on the right track.

That internal struggle is not a sign you should avoid the task, but it signals you need to approach it using the skills you learned in the previous chapter: noticing and naming each of the emotions, rules, and reasons as they happen.

You need to say yes to your internal struggle and lean into it, all the way! You need to use the noticing and naming skills you learned in Chapter 5, Compassionate Accountability. You need to commit to making room for the uneasiness that accompanies living your values.

ACTIVITY: Using your values-based goals and actions to tackle procrastination

Consider a project you want to accomplish today and go through each of the prompts below.

Something you usually procrastinate over is:

. . . .

. . . .

This activity matters to you because (note something you care about):

. . . .

. . . .

You values based goals are:

. . . .

. . . .

The feelings and sensations you need to notice and name are:

. . . .

. . . .

· ·

· ·

The rules and reasons you need to notice and name are:

· ·

· ·

· ·

· ·

The self-doubt and negative stories you need to make room for are:

· ·

· ·

· ·

· ·

The minimizing thoughts you need to watch for are:

· ·

· ·

· ·

· ·

Moving forward, you can use these prompts as a guide for any activity you want to take care of.

WRAPPING UP

Instead of pursuing outcome goals, getting trapped in emotional goals, or pursuing mid-term priorities, you can specify actionable steps that are under your control and in alignment with your values.

Ask yourself, as often as possible: "What concrete steps can I take right now toward building a life I love?"

You can make every step count in overcoming procrastinating habits!

CHAPTER 7

WORKING SKILLFULLY WITH A CLOCKLESS MIND

Julian, a law student, has the following go-to routine when working on an assignment. As he prepares to start working on it two weeks before the deadline, his mind—a good glitchy helper—thinks: "I don't need to do anything right now; I entered this assignment into my calendar so I'll remember it. I deserve a break before working on another project."

It doesn't matter what the subject is, whether he is interested in it or not, or whether he has the time to work on it or not. He gets hooked on the reasons to put the assignment off.

The day before the deadline, usually around 11 p.m. or midnight, Julian goes into urgency mode: he frantically types and pulls an all-nighter to finish the assignment. He knows he could have done better, but he was in desperation mode trying to get it done.

"Sometimes, I manage to turn in the paper and get an okay grade; other times, I don't make it on time."

Richard, a mechanic, wants to take care of his regular tasks at home and work but would also love to branch out and try new projects, play new sports, learn new skills, organize gatherings with friends, and have some fun. His attention and time are pulled in so many directions that it's hard for him to figure out how to do things. He doesn't know how other people do it!

A well-lived life requires time management.

This chapter is about time management but not the type of time management you expect; think of this chapter as an ACTifying approach to time management.

When I searched for "time management" books on Amazon, a webpage with 33 book recommendations loaded on my screen. When I looked at the bottom of the page, 49 more pages were waiting to be reviewed. Clearly, in the information era, we have been very preoccupied with making the best of our time, being productive, and using hacks to take care of our chores.

There's nothing wrong with wanting to make the best use of your time; that makes sense given the busyness of your life, your responsibilities, and the many roles you play in your relationships, career, work, community, and spiritual circles.

However, the time-management tools that are supposed to free up your time can also make you more anxious, more concerned, and more worried about how you spend your time. The same tools that are supposed to open your schedule to do more fun, leisurely, and creative activities can pull you into overthinking, overplanning, and overpreparing, especially if you're prone to perfectionism.

Consider the notion of "inbox zero." For years, responding to your emails as soon as possible and reaching "inbox zero" was like a badge of honor in business, academic settings, writing communities, and other groups. On social media you may have seen your friends posting about cleaning their inboxes, receiving many virtual hearts of acknowledgment.

However, becoming efficient at responding to emails doesn't always mean you're prioritizing what truly matters to you; quite likely, most emails you receive are important, yes, but not all of them are related to your personal values or enrich your life in the long run.

Being exposed to one-size-fits-all productivity messages makes your mind vulnerable to unworkable comparisons. You may find yourself measuring your productivity against someone else's, even though your circumstances are different from what others are going through. Moreover, while it's easy to admire people who seem to get things done promptly, we don't know what is happening behind the scenes in their lives. Productivity looks different for each of us.

Time management has become an approach for doing more, faster, and better. But—feel free to highlight the next sentence!—the key is to get faster and better at doing the things that move you closer to being who you want to be without ignoring what's happening in your life, chronically exhausting your body, ignoring the people who matter, or getting hooked by the productivity trap.

How do you relate to time? When you think about the notion of "time in your life," what first comes to your mind?

. . . .

. . . .

. . . .

. . . .

I'm going to take a wild guess here and say that you, like me, feel stressed about time. You, like many people, may have a large pile of books to read, podcast episodes to listen to, or long lists of movies to watch that you've been meaning to get around to... if only you had the time.

It's not that you're doing anything wrong; we often forget that time is a limited resource in our life. It moves forward, non-stop.

This may sound so obvious, yet, the amount that we try to fit in during a day, the extent to which we're encouraged to do more and more, and how much we hustle, suggest that we live under the impression that we can control time.

Radically accepting that, every day you're alive, you have a finite number of hours to show up to life as you want to and live your values—without adding unnecessary stress—is the beginning of a helpful relationship with time.

Let's examine two common beliefs about time that people get hooked on when needing to take care of things.

YOUR TWO OLD BUDDIES

You're probably familiar with the thoughts about time that pop up in your mind when you're dealing with deadlines or starting to tackle your to-do list. I won't ask you to list all of them but to focus on two categories that reinforce your procrastination habits: "I do things better under pressure" and "I know how much time it's going to take me to get this done."

Old buddy: "But I do things better under pressure."
Let's start with a brief activity.

ACTIVITY: How do you relate to deadlines in general?

Imagine a time-sensitive report at work or school that you knew two months in advance you needed to complete.

How did you think of the time leading up to this task's due date?

. . . .

. . . .

. . . .

. . . .

How did you think about this project and its deadline seven weeks out?

....

....

....

....

What were your thoughts about the timeline and this project three weeks out?

....

....

....

....

Five days out?

....

....

....

....

Ten hours out?

....

....

....

....

Your mind will probably tell you things like, "I perform much better with a deadline; the rush helps me concentrate and I usually have more focused attention; when I'm chasing adrenaline, I can do better."

Let's step back and check the data. Different studies in sports and educational psychology have demonstrated that there are optimal levels of arousal in learning and performance. In some sports—like wrestling, rugby or jiujitsu—athletes require high levels of arousal to play at their best. Other sports—including golf and tennis—require more precision, so players do better with low levels of arousal.

These are known as "zones of optimal functioning." The theory suggests that athletes need an optimal level of anxiety—either low, medium, or high—at which they perform their best (Gould and Tuffey 1996). Smith (1990) refers to "optimal arousal" as a level of mental stimulation at which physical performance, learning, or temporary feelings of well-being are maximized.

With cognitive tasks, time pressure makes you work faster but not necessarily better. As Moore and Tenney (2012) state, "time pressure generally impairs performance because it places constraints on the capacity for thought and action that limit exploration and increase reliance on well-learned or heuristic strategies. Thus, time pressure increases speed at the expense of quality."

I hear you saying, "But Dr. Z., when I'm anxious I can focus better, believe it or not."

While it's possible that, at times, anxiety could be feeding into what you pay attention to when completing a time-sensitive project, you should check how this approach works for you in your life in general and in the long run.

How does it feel to be in a rush, always doing things last minute, waking up after barely sleeping a few hours, rushing to do good-enough work, and knowing it doesn't reflect your full competence?

Yes, you can be more productive and get a task done when you're under time pressure and when feeling that urgency, that adrenaline. But you're sacrificing, compromising and putting at risk the quality of your performance and your well-being in the long run.

Old buddy: "I know how much time it takes me to get things done."

In your everyday life, you estimate mundane tasks like doing laundry, cleaning, taking a class at the gym, working on this workbook, or going grocery shopping; you also plan for more complex activities like preparing for a job interview, paying taxes, putting together a dinner for your friends, planning your wedding, or organizing your next vacation.

We all need to estimate how long certain tasks will take to complete, and how much time we have left to do them. The question is, how do you actually allocate time for the tasks you need to finish?

ACTIVITY: Acknowledging your miscalculations

Think about five times when there was a mismatch between the time you estimated for a task and the time it actually took you to complete it. Jot down the tasks, estimated time, and actual time.

Task 1

. . . .

. . . .

. . . .

. . . .

. . . .

Task 2

. . . .

. . . .

....

....

....

Task 3

....

....

....

....

....

Task 4

....

....

....

....

....

Task 5

....

....

....

....

....

If you have a history of procrastination behaviors, you know you have a complicated relationship with time. You underestimate the time it will take you to get a large project done and may overestimate how long it will take you to complete a small task.

This way of thinking is known as the *planning fallacy* or *optimistic thinking*. The planning fallacy describes your tendency to be overly optimistic about time and your mind's proneness to minimizing costs or potential obstacles when getting things done.

To free yourself from the shackles of procrastination behaviors, be aware of these two common old buddies:

- I do things better under pressure.
- I know how much time it takes.

When having these thoughts, I encourage you to respond to them as you would to any unhelpful thoughts that pop up in your mind: notice them, acknowledge them, and make room for them; you can even say, "Hello, my old and dear friends; thanks for visiting me." You don't need to challenge or question them. After noticing and naming these familiar thoughts, do your best to choose an action that takes you closer to your values.

Every time you notice and name unhelpful thoughts, you get better and better at choosing your behaviors instead of making feeling-good choices or being run over by every unhelpful thought that shows up in your mind.

In the next sections, you will learn about other practical skills to working flexibly with time. Take notes, highlight what stands out, and try these skills. Make this section yours!

CONDUCTING A VALUES-BASED TIME AUDIT

I learned about time management in grad school; it was impossible to move forward in the program without tracking how I was spending my time. When

I was introduced to ACT, I became much more vigilant about whether I was devoting time to activities that took me closer to my values or not.

Over the last ten years, here is something I have done (and every time-management book will encourage you to do this too): a time audit!

The word "audit" sounds annoying to our ears, I get it. It can feel overwhelming to even think about managing time better, let alone doing an audit. But here's the thing: time audits aren't about being perfect or making yourself feel guilty. They're just a way to get curious about where your time is really going.

I'm not a happy camper when I'm reviewing my time. Yet, the benefits of performing a time audit are extraordinary.

I started doing these once a year and then, later on, at the beginning and in the middle of the year. There have also been times when I felt pulled in so many directions that I knew I needed to check how I was really spending my time more often than twice a year. These days, I do a values-based time audit every quarter.

ACTIVITY: Examining your time with your eyes open!

Set aside a week for this activity before continuing to the next section in this chapter. No cheating!

Here is what you need to do:

- Keep track of your daily activities and how much time each one of them takes you. Use any form of log you want, don't overthink it, and don't make it complicated for yourself. Just make sure you're using the same log every day. You can track your activities on a piece of paper, your calendar, or elsewhere.

- Don't guess. Don't try to complete your log at the end of the day because you will forget things and that defeats the purpose of your time audit.

Keep track of those big activities—in my case, working with clients, cooking, exercising—as well as the tasks that may seem mundane—returning calls, checking and writing emails, doing the laundry. Don't skip commuting time if you have to drive somewhere.

- After tracking your activities for a week, grab your time log, read the prompts below, and answer them.
  - Which activities relate to your values?
  - Which activities are time wasters?
  - Which values-based activities are time-sensitive and urgent?
  - Which activities are soothing and relaxing for you?

Not knowing what activities you spend time on can often lead you to a range of problems. You might treat checking emails as pressing and end up spending hours on them. You may underestimate how long it will take to cook dinner or complete a work project. You may be approaching everything as urgent, jumping from task to task without a clear plan, minimizing the time constraints of some tasks, and ignoring your values more often than you realize.

If one of your core values is learning new stuff, but you're constantly procrastinating on activities like reading or taking new workshops because you're caught up in putting out fires, it's easy to feel disconnected and frustrated.

When considering each activity in relationship to your values, some tasks may feel mundane and unrelated to the life you want to live. If so, don't quickly ignore them. Instead, remember to ask yourself the questions from the section "What's the point?" in Chapter 3, Finding the Compass of Your Life.

ORGANIZING STRATEGIC TO-DO LISTS

We all have some form of to-do list for taking care of chores, projects, and tasks we need to accomplish. How long is your list? How does it feel when you look at it?

Most people suffering with procrastinating habits have long lists. When a list contains too many tasks, it can trigger a psychological phenomenon known as the "Zeigarnik effect," where incomplete tasks occupy mental space, creating a sense of unease and urgency that can actually impair focus and productivity (Baumeister and Vohs 2007).

A long list defeats the purpose of keeping you organized.

To overcome the pitfalls of having a long to-do list, Oliver Burkeman (2021) recommends keeping two strategic to-do lists.

ACTIVITY: Creating your two to-do lists

Follow the directions below to create two separate lists. Make sure to use action verbs for each item in both lists.

- First list: Jot down every single activity, regardless of size or feasibility, that you need to complete to align your actions with your values in all areas of your life. It doesn't matter how small or overwhelming the activity seems, simply record it on this first list. Think of this list as a comprehensive container for everything you must complete.

  This is the list you will be using to capture every new project that arises.

- Second list: Create a second list that includes only time-sensitive tasks or projects with firm deadlines. Keep this list to seven items or fewer.

  This is more of a closed list, and you should review it no more than once a week.

- Commit to moving an item from your first list, the open list—which contains all activities—to the second, closed list only after you have checked off a task from the second list.

  Don't add any new tasks to your second list until a space opens up by completing a task from it.

This strategy of maintaining two distinct to-do lists, an open one and a focused closed to-do list, offers you several advantages: it helps you to prioritize tasks, takes into consideration the limited amount of time and resources you have, enhances your productivity, reduces decision fatigue, keeps you accountable, and improves your overall well-being.

ORGANIZING YOUR TIME WITH FOUR KEY PRINCIPLES

After my TEDx talk "Stop playing-it-safe and start living" got released, I received a couple of messages from former and current clients. They all had one question for me: How do you organize your time?

Organizing your time is about living your values seasonally and humbly.

Here are four principles for you to keep in mind when organizing your time.

First principle: Adding 25 percent more

When looking at your values-based activities, expect your mind to tell you, "You have time, there's no need to rush, it won't take too long," or "You work better last minute." Remember those old friends we addressed at the beginning of this chapter?

Our minds do mindy things all the time, don't they?

Look at your second to-do list, your closed list that includes time-sensitive projects, and block time for each item, but with one key adjustment: Estimate how long you think each task will take and then add about 25 percent more time to it. This extra buffer will help you to avoid last-minute stress (Andreou and White 2010).

Second principle: Scheduling annoying tasks

Despite your best intentions to focus on your values, you will still encounter tasks that are annoying, frustrating, and hard to check off from your first to-do list. These are the tasks you need to make sure don't slip off your weekly schedule.

Professor David Premack (1959) formulated the Premack principle, a behavioral approach to pairing a highly probable behavior (something you already do) with a less probable behavior (something you tend to avoid). The Premack principle is foundational to another skill for tackling procrastination: temptation building (Milkman, Minson, and Volpp 2014) or habit stacking (Clear 2018).

Essentially, to make the "should" tasks more doable or to build new habits, you need to combine an activity you find challenging with one you already do, without compromising the quality of any of either task.

You're more likely to start chipping away at tasks you've been avoiding if you get to do them while simultaneously doing one of your favorite things. For example, if you have been postponing going for a 30-minute walk, commit to going for a walk while listening to your favorite songs or podcast. This way, you make it more likely for you to follow through with activities you struggle tackling.

Some tasks require your full attention and shouldn't be combined with any other activity. If you are struggling to respond to work emails and try to do so while watching your favorite TV show, the quality of your replies will be compromised.

Third principle: Scheduling a weekly review

It's very important that, at the beginning of your week, you book at least 30 minutes to go over your weekly calendar, look at your values-based second list, and rearrange items as required.

Sometimes people are averse to scheduling because it can feel restrictive, as if organizing your calendar is putting yourself in jail and limiting your freedom to do spontaneous things.

If this sounds like you, I encourage you to consider that scheduling is not just about allotting a chunk of time to specific activities. It's also about intentionally deciding *not* to do other things that take you further from the person you aspire to be.

If you don't organize your time, two things will happen:

1. You will struggle to decide how to spend time. Your mind will come up with questions like: What should I do now? Should I take care of taxes or go grocery shopping?
2. You may find yourself hopping between tasks or getting sidetracked by small, unplanned activities.

Multitasking can feel productive at times, but the research shows it often reduces efficiency and the quality of your work (Ophir, Nass, and Wagner 2009). The only scenarios where multitasking can be helpful to you are when you're mixing an automatic task with a low-effort cognitive task.

Not planning how to spend your time leads you to distraction and to procrastination.

Scheduling your week and reviewing it may feel mechanical at first. However, to avoid letting time pass you by, floating through life and living reactively, I invite you to gently acknowledge any initial distress, focus on your values, and give making time to plan and organize your week a try.

Fourth principle: Squeezing less!

Let me briefly share Raj and Peter's evening:

On a Monday evening, Raj and Peter got together for dinner; they went to their favorite vegan restaurant in the city. To their surprise, there was a long wait list. They added their name, knowing that the food was good so the wait was worthwhile. The waiter, in a firm and friendly tone, told them, "You will have a table in 45 minutes."

Raj and Peter smiled and went outside. As they stood on the street, Raj noticed a spa across the street, turned to Peter, and asked, "Should we go get a half-hour massage?"

When I shared this story with a friend, they asked, "Patricia, what's your point? These two seem to be making good use of an unexpected chunk of downtime."

Our minds are so tricky. Have you been in my friend's shoes? Trying to do more and more every minute that opens up in your schedule?

It may seem very practical to dash across the street and get a massage, but even if everything went perfectly—no waiting line, an efficient receptionist, and an immediate start of the massage—it would still mean changing clothes twice, rushing back to dinner, and hoping you didn't miss your reservation.

The key to breaking the pattern of procrastination is not to cram more into your schedule, but to intentionally do *less*, focusing on what really matters to you within the limited time you have.

You may want to connect with your friend on Friday evening but know that if you do, you won't finish your paper. You may want to watch a new movie but then won't have a chance to hang out with your neighbor.

Instead of adding and adding and adding activities onto your plate, choose to prioritize one or two areas of your life every week. One week you could focus on your relationships and career, the next on your career and health, and so on.

You can live intentionally and without adding the unnecessary stress that comes with trying to do too much.

ACTIVITY: Scheduling your week!

Take a moment to gather both of your strategic to-do lists and any weekly calendar you use to keep track of your time. Plan your week following these key principles:

- adding 25 percent extra time
- scheduling a weekly review
- squeezing in less
- scheduling annoying tasks.

Following these principles will help you live with intention, without juggling too many plates.

WRAPPING UP

Time management isn't a question of how perfectly you optimize every second of your day, or the app you use to keep track of tasks, or how fast you do things.

It's about creating a life you love and are proud of, not just a checklist.

In this chapter, I invite you to acknowledge the constraints of time and accept the disappointment that can come when making values-based choices.

Choosing which values-based activities you say yes and no to is one of the hardest challenges you'll face. As much as you would love to, it's impossible to live your values perfectly: this is just part of being human.

You cannot do everything, but you can choose to get something meaningful done every day; something that, over time, helps you grow a joyful life.

Take a deep breath, be kind to yourself, and try out the skills from this chapter.

Plan a week that honors you and the life you want to build with the finite amount of time you have each day.

CHAPTER 8

DOING THE DOING WITH A FOCUSED MIND

Quite often, when my friends and clients are doing their best to change their procrastination habits, they share things like:

- "I was getting ready to shop for groceries for the weekend and it occurred to me to take a sneak peek of my Instagram feed, a tiny one. An hour passed and I was still looking at my IG."
- "I was ready to prepare documents to do my taxes, found a postcard from my ex-girlfriend, and next thing, I'm searching for more stuff I had from her so I can keep it all in the same place."
- "A tiny task feels so big; suddenly, it's a lot to do. How bad would it be to catch up on a group chat right now?"
- "I started working on that report and couldn't keep up with it. I got distracted by the song playing on my Spotify."
- "I was typing on my laptop and then I remembered how much I'm paying for cable TV, so I texted my neighbors asking about other cable companies."

Starting a task and staying focused on a project can be very challenging in the mind of a procrastinator. It's not that you don't like the idea of doing things and completing tasks; it's just that when you sit down to knock out a task, your tricky mind pops up with a lot of stuff that pushes your attention in a different direction. Ayayay with our minds!

The skills you learned in Chapters 3–7 have shown you how to effectively manage each one of the distressing internal experiences or psychological processes that keep you postponing your life: cozy rules, familiar reasons, minimizing thoughts, uneasy feelings, uncomfortable sensations, critical self, feeling-good choices, and disconnection from your values.

In this chapter, we'll go over micro-skills for managing distractibility. I won't overwhelm you with hundreds of pages on techniques, apps, or tips to remain focused. Instead, I'll share with you the most important skills and principles that will help you stay centered.

What makes it hard for you to stay focused on a task?

. . . .

. . . .

. . . .

. . . .

. . . .

. . . .

. . . .

. . . .

You're not alone. It's hard not to get distracted these days. Chances are that while completing this workbook you paused to check your social media, play with your kitty, answer a text or make a dinner reservation. That's completely normal!

In fact, research shows that our attention spans have been decreasing over the years due to constant digital interruptions. A study conducted by Mark and colleagues (2015) found that people switch tasks on average every three minutes and five seconds, often due to external interruptions like notifications or internal triggers such as boredom or curiosity.

You need to develop new habits to minimize the long distracting detours your mind takes, increase focused time, and get better at completing activities that matter to you.

GETTING READY TO FOCUS

Cal Newport (2016), in his book *Deep Work: Rules for Focused Success in a Distracted World*, suggests that the best-performing students are not the ones working longer hours, but those who can create intense focus. Fascinating, right?

Newport coined the term "deep work" to refer to a person's capacity for focused, high-quality activities, free from distractions.

Here are some principles to help you create your own deep work sessions.

Revisiting your values and goals

As soon as you start a task, ask yourself the following questions:

- What's the activity I will work on?
- How long will I work for?
- How will that activity contribute to my life in the long run?
- How will I support myself when I'm done with this activity?

Answering these prompts is a powerful reminder of what you're committing to do and why it's important to you.

ACTIVITY: Writing down your personal commitment

After answering these questions, write down your personal commitment using the template below, and place it in a visible place in your work area.

Personal commitment:

Today [day, time] . . . . I'll do [activity you will

work on] . . . .

. . . .   for [enter the time] . . . .

in the service of [your personal values] . . . .

. . . .

. . . .

Making this commitment isn't about doing things perfectly, it's about being intentional about doing what matters.

Removing environmental distractions

This may sound very simple, but it's often overlooked and hard to do. Gloria Mark and colleagues (2008) found that the average American worker gets distracted approximately every three minutes. And, when a person gets interrupted, it takes an average of 23 minutes to return to focus on the original task. Isn't that mind-blowing?

It's like everything around you is competing for your attention and, on top of that, you are pulled in different directions because of your feelings, thoughts, images, dreams, rules, reasons, and other internal distractions. No wonder staying focused can feel like a battle!

The more you get distracted with stuff, the more opportunities you miss to move forward in life. You need to be intentional about removing environmental distractions, such as notifications, cell phones, and TVs.

ACTIVITY: Make an inventory of the distracting items

Be intentional about making a list of all objects or devices that distract your attention which you need to remove from your working area.

. . . .

. . . .

. . . .

. . . .

. . . .

. . . .

. . . .

. . . .

By creating a space free of distractions, you're setting yourself up for deep focus work, so you can give your full attention to what really counts.

You deserve that kind of focus!

Approaching complex tasks

When looking at your values-based to-do lists, you will likely find tasks that feel too lengthy or overwhelming to complete right away. Naturally you have strong urges to put them off, and that's completely understandable. Your mind is just doing what it knows best: procrastinating.

In a comprehensive review, Steel (2007) explored the nature of procrastination and found that people are more likely to delay tasks that are perceived as difficult, ambiguous, or lacking in structure. Steel noted that procrastination is closely linked to the concept of "temporal discounting," where the immediate benefits of avoiding a complex task—for example, feeling relieved or relaxed—outweigh the long-term benefits of completing it.

Instead of falling into the same old postponing patterns, you can pre-pare to skillfully approach these complex tasks. The following activity will guide you on how you can tackle complex projects step-by-step without getting lost.

ACTIVITY: Visualizing the most overwhelming tasks

Choose a task that feels overwhelming. Break it down by writing out the different steps that the task requires. Don't worry if the step is too big or small, just write down all the steps involved to complete this task.

Read through the directions below so you know what to do next before you start.

If you feel comfortable, close your eyes or focus your gaze on a single point. Start visualizing the first step required to complete this task, imagining yourself completing it in as much detail as possible. Watch this scene as if you're watching a movie.

As you hold on to this image in your mind, notice the feelings, sensations, and thoughts that come with it.

Stay with this image for a couple of moments. Watch your mind. If a ruling thought pops up, label it as "rule." If you notice a reason-giving thought, label it "reason." If your critical self shows up, acknowledge it as you did in Chapter 5, Compassionate Accountability. You can even say, "Hello, my old friend, Mr. Criticism!"

Notice and name those internal experiences. See what your glitchy helper does. You can also say, "I notice this [feeling, sensation, thought]." Without judging yourself or those internal experiences, without trying to understand why you're feeling or thinking that way, watch them as they come and go without arguing with, replacing, or rushing through them. Just watch them as they happen.

Keep focusing on the initial feeling or sensation that you recognized in that first scene for at least two to three minutes, without rushing. If you notice a new feeling showing up, take a deep breath, open your eyes, and ground yourself in the moment. Press your feet against the floor for a few seconds.

Now look at the next steps you wrote down, then move to the next scene and repeat the same process. Keep visualizing the steps this task involves until you finish visualizing all the actions, even when it feels repetitive, tedious, or simplistic.

You can use these skills together—noticing, naming, and visualizing a complex task—any time you need to tackle a task with multiple steps. Each time you visualize the required actions, and notice and name those internal reactions your mind comes up with for each step, you're breaking those procrastinating habits and building new ones.

COMPASSIONATE COACHING WHEN TACKLING PROJECTS

Watching your mind is a very, very, very valuable skill in all situations. I personally think of it as an essential life skill; so much shows up in our minds, and many negative scripts run either in the background or right in the foreground of everything we do. No exceptions!

When checking off items from your to-do lists, you should expect your mind to get busy telling you how difficult the task is, convincing you of negative outcomes, or commanding you to choose something much more fun instead.

You can gently nudge yourself into action by connecting with your compassionate self and imagining yourself hearing short, encouraging catchphrases like:

- It's challenging to do this, and it matters to me.
- Every project starts with action after action.
- This is tough, but I'm showing up because it matters to me.
- It feels uncomfortable now, and I know it's important to do this.

- Step by step, I'm making a meaningful difference in the long run.
- Little by little makes a difference in the long run.
- Every task starts with small and consistent actions.
- I don't feel great right now, but every effort is a step toward my values.

You would benefit from coming up with your own personal encouraging statements that resonate with you.

ACTIVITY: What's your compassionate encouraging statement?

How can you encourage yourself to continue tackling projects that matter to you?

Take a moment to think about phrases that motivate you and write them down. Make sure these statements don't focus on trying to feel good or less stressed; instead, let them acknowledge your struggle and remind you that the struggle is worthy.

....

....

....

....

....

....

....

....

....

....

Being compassionate with yourself is not a random act of gentleness, but a way to stay connected with what truly matters without attacking yourself.

STAYING FOCUSED

When you're awake, you're paying attention to something. The question is whether you're paying attention to things that expand your life or drain it. Consider your regular day: If you're watching a series on Netflix, talking to your partner, cooking a meal, riding your bike, or reading a book, you're paying attention to something.

Think of your attention as a spotlight that you're in charge of (even when it doesn't feel like it).

Staying focused means intentionally paying attention to what matters in a given moment, keeping the attention there, and redirecting it as many times as needed when your mind wanders.

Here are a few tips to stay focused:

- Watch the remarks your mind makes in a detached way.
- Acknowledge those thoughts by saying something like, "Interesting thought," or, "Here goes another distracting thought."
- Don't analyze or try to prove those thoughts wrong. Just acknowledge them and keep doing what you're doing.

ACTIVITY: Noticing your distracting thoughts

How would you respond to distracting thoughts in a detached manner?

. . . .

. . . .

....

....

....

....

....

....

WRAPPING UP

The information era asks so much of your mind, and cultivating a focused mind can truly transform every aspect of your life.

As you try out the skills from this chapter, I encourage you to ease into practicing them without chasing a quick fix. By intentionally practicing these skills, you're not just learning how to stay focused when approaching tasks; you're learning a far more valuable life skill: the art of living purposefully while getting things done!

Appendix

ONLINE CLASSES

I have created online classes that teach practical, hands-on acceptance and commitment skills for managing ineffective playing-it-safe moves related anxiety, perfectionism, procrastination, phobias, worry, and OCD.

These online resources are designed to offer you flexibility and access to the material at anytime that works best for you, allowing you to learn at your pace, at a time that fits with your schedule, and from the comfort of your home.

Each recorded class builds on the content of my books; expanding it further with experiential exercises, worksheets, and additional skills to dive deeper into addressing specific challenges.

More information: www.thisisdoctorz.com.

WORKING WITH DR. Z.

I love working with overachievers and overthinkers to get them unstuck from worries, fears, anxieties, obsessions, perfectionism, procrastination, and ineffective playing-it-safe actions.

A key question to my work is, "How can we get unstuck from ineffective playing-it-safe moves so we can live a meaningful, fulfilling, and purposeful life?" To answer that question, I do my best to share skills and principles derived from behavioral science—Acceptance and Commitment Therapy, social psychology, and organizational psychology—in a way that is uncomplicated, unpretentious, and as real as it gets.

You can work with me individually in two ways: (1) therapy or (2) coaching.

If you're interested in therapy or coaching, go to this website: www.eastbaybehaviortherapycenter.com

BOOKS WRITTEN BY DR. Z.

Zurita Ona, P. (2022). *The ACT Acceptance and Commitment Skills for Perfectionism and High-Achieving Behaviors*. London: Routledge.

Zurita Ona, P. (2020). *Living Beyond OCD: Using Acceptance and Commitment Therapy and Exposure Skills*. London: Routledge.

Zurita Ona, P. (2019). *ACT Workbook for Teens with OCD: Unhook Yourself and Live Life to the Full*. London: Jessica Kingsley Publishers.

Zurita Ona, P. (2019). *ACT for Borderline Personality Disorder: A Flexible Treatment Plan for Clients with Emotion Dysregulation*. Oakland, CA: New Harbinger.

Zurita Ona, P. (2018). *Escaping the Emotional Roller Coaster: Acceptance and Commitment Therapy for the Emotionally Sensitive*. Chatswood, NSW: Exisle Publishing.

Zurita Ona, P. (2017). *Parenting a Troubled Teen: Deal with Intense Emotions and Stop Conflict Using Acceptance and Commitment Therapy*. Oakland, CA: New Harbinger.

McKay, M., Fanning, P., and Zurita Ona, P. (2011). *Mind and Emotions*. Oakland, CA: New Harbinger.

NEWSLETTER

If you want to receive weekly tips to help break free from procrastination, perfectionism, worries, obsessions, fears, anxiety, and other ineffective playing-it-safe moves, you can subscribe to my free weekly newsletter, Playing-It-Safe.

I would love for you to join me! Go to this website and sign up: www.thisisdoctorz.com/playing-it-safe-newsletter.

Every other Wednesday I share a single tip with all subscribers. When you sign up, you receive exclusive, free, and specialized content.

TEDX TALK

If you want to uncover how "playing-it-safe" moves might be quietly shaping your life, I invite you to watch my 17-minute TEDx talk: "Stop playing-it-safe and start living!" You can find it on YouTube!

PODCAST

The Playing-it-Safe podcast features both solo episodes and conversations with other experts to unpack anxiety-based reactions and ineffective playing-it-safe moves that are holding you back.

Each episode is grounded in my work with clients and contextual behavioral science. I do my best to provide you with practical tools to live a joyful and meaningful life.

You can tune in on your favorite podcast platform or catch episodes at www.playingitsafe.zone.

PROFESSIONAL CONSULTATION

I offer ongoing consultation to professionals interested in learning the applications of ACT for specific anxiety-based struggles, such as perfectionism, procrastination, OCD, anxiety, worry, phobias, trauma, and emotion regulation.

More information: www.thisisdoctorz.com.

SPEAKING ENGAGEMENTS

I love giving presentations that are jargon-free, full of hands-on skills to put into action right away, and with many insights from current behavioral science and social psychology.

The overall motto of my presentations can be summarized in this sentence, "less talking, more practicing, and more living."

More information: www.thisisdoctorz.com.

References

Andreou, C. and White, M.D. (2010). *The Thief of Time*. Oxford: Oxford University Press.

Basco, M.R. (2009). *The Procrastinator's Guide to Getting Things Done*. New York: Guilford Press.

Baumeister, R.F. and Vohs, K.D. (2007). *Encyclopedia of Social Psychology*. London: SAGE.

Baumeister, R.F., Vohs, K.D., Aaker, J.L, and Garbinsky, E.N. (2013). Some key differences between a happy life and a meaningful life. *Journal of Positive Psychology, 8*(6), 505–516.

Borkovec, T.D., Ray, W.J., and Stöber, J. (1998). Worry: A cognitive phenomenon intimately linked to affective, physiological, and interpersonal behavioral processes. *Cognitive Therapy and Research, 22*(6), 561–576. https://doi.org/10.1023/A:1018790003416

Burka, J.B. and Yuen, L.M. (1983). *Procrastination: Why You Do It, What to Do About It*. Reading, MA: Addison Wesley.

Breines, J.G. and Chen, S. (2012). Self-compassion increases self-improvement motivation. *Personality and Social Psychology Bulletin, 38*(9), 1133–1143.

Burkeman, O. (2021). *Four Thousand Weeks: Time Management for Mortals*. New York: Farrar, Straus, and Giroux.

Clear, J. (2018). *Atomic Habits: An Easy and Proven Way to Build Good Habits and Break Bad Ones*. New York: Avery.

Ferrari, J.R. and Tice, D.M. (2000). Procrastination as a self-handicap for men and women: A task avoidance strategy in a laboratory setting. *Journal of Research in Personality, 34*(1), 73–83.

Feyzi Behnagh, R. and Ferrari, J.R. (2022). Exploring 40 years on affective correlates to procrastination: A literature review of situational and dispositional types. *Current Psychology, 41*(2), 1097–1111. https://doi.org/10.1007/s12144-021-02653-z

Gilbert, P. (2009). *The Compassionate Mind: A New Approach to Life's Challenges*. London: Constable.

Gilbert, P. and Choden (2014). *Mindful Compassion: How the Science of Compassion Can Help You Understand Your Emotions, Live in the Present, and Connect Deeply with Others*. Oakland, CA: New Harbinger.

Gould, D. and Tuffey, S. (1996). Zones of optimal functioning research: A review and critique. *Anxiety, Stress & Coping, 9*(1), 53–68. https://doi.org/10.1080/10615809608249392

Hayes, S.C., Bond, F.W., Barnes-Holmes, D., and Austin, J. (eds) (2006). *Acceptance and*

Mindfulness at Work: Applying Acceptance and Commitment Therapy and Relational Frame Theory to Organizational Behavior Management. Binghamton, NY: Raworth Press.

Kim, H. (2005). Self-criticism as a safety behavior: Implications for social anxiety and depression. *Journal of Cognitive Psychotherapy, 19*(4), 415–428.

Kolts, R.L. (2016). *CFT Made Simple: A Clinician's Guide to Practicing Compassion-Focused Therapy.* Oakland, CA: New Harbinger.

Leary, M.R., Tate, E.B., Adams, C.E., Allen, A.B., and Hancock, J. (2007). Self-compassion and reactions to unpleasant self-relevant events: The implications of treating oneself kindly. *Journal of Personality and Social Psychology, 92*(5), 887–904.

Lyubomirsky, S., King, L, and Diener, E. (2005). The benefits of frequent positive affect: Does happiness lead to success? *Psychological Bulletin, 131*(6), 803–855.

Mark, G., Gudith, D., and Klocke, U. (2008). The cost of interrupted work: More speed and stress. *Proceedings of the SIGCHI Conference on Human Factors in Computing Systems,* 107–110. https://doi.org/10.1145/1357054.1357072

Mark, G., Iqbal, S.T., Czerwinski, M., Johns, P, and Sano, A. (2015). Neurotics can't focus: An in situ study of online multitasking in the workplace. *Proceedings of the 18th ACM Conference on Computer Supported Cooperative Work & Social Computing,* 173–185. https://doi.org/10.1145/2675133.2675193

Marshall, S.L., Parker, P.D., Ciarrochi, J., Sahdra, B., Jackson, C.J., and Heaven, P.C.L. (2015). Self-compassion protects against the negative effects of low self-esteem: A longitudinal study in a large adolescent sample. *Personality and Individual Differences, 74,* 116–121.

Milkman, K.L., Minson, J.A, and Volpp, K.G.M. (2014). Holding the hunger games hostage at the gym: An evaluation of temptation bundling. *Management Science, 60*(2), 283–299. https://doi.org/10.1287/mnsc.2013.1784

Moore, D.A. and Tenney, E.R. (2012). Time pressure, performance, and productivity. *Research on Managing Groups and Teams, 15,* 305–326. https://doi.org/10.1108/s1534-0856(2012)0000015015

Neely, M.E., Schallert, D.L., Mohammed, S.S., Roberts, R.M., and Chen, Y.J. (2009). Self-kindness when facing stress: The role of self-compassion, goal regulation, and support in college students' well-being. *Motivation and Emotion, 33*(1), 88–97.

Newport, C. (2016). *Deep Work: Rules for Focused Success in a Distracted World.* London: Piatkus Books.

Ophir, E., Nass, C., and Wagner, A.D. (2009). Cognitive control in media multitaskers. *Proceedings of the National Academy of Sciences, 106*(37), 15583–15587.

Premack, D. (1959). Toward empirical behavior laws: I. Positive reinforcement. *Psychological Review, 66*(4), 219–233.

Pychyl, T.A., Morin, R.W., and Salmon, B.R. (2000). Procrastination and planning fallacy: An examination of the study habits of university students. *Journal of Social Behavior and Personality, 15,* 135–150.

Ramsay, J.R. (2020). The moderating effect of attention-deficit hyperactivity disorder symptoms on the relationship between procrastination and internalizing symptoms in the general adult population. *Frontiers in Psychology, 11,* Article 505.

Salkovskis, P.M. (1996). The Cognitive Approach to Anxiety: Threat Beliefs, Safety-Seeking

Behavior, and the Special Case of Health Anxiety and Obsessions. In P.M. Salkovskis (Ed.), *Frontiers of Cognitive Therapy*. New York: Guilford Press.

Sirois, F.M. (2014). Procrastination and stress: Exploring the role of self-compassion. *Self and Identity, 13*(2), 128–145. https://doi.org/10.1080/152.2013.763404

Sirois, F.M. (2023). Procrastination and stress: A conceptual review of why context matters. *International Journal of Environmental Research and Public Health, 20*(6), 5031. https://doi.org/10.3390/ijerph20065031

Smith, S.L. (1990). *Dictionary of Concepts in Recreation and Leisure Studies*. Westport, CT: Greenwood.

Steel, P. (2007). The nature of procrastination: A meta-analytic and theoretical review of quintessential self-regulatory failure. *Psychological Bulletin, 133*(1), 65–94. doi: 10.1037/0033-2909.133.1.65. PMID: 17201571.

Thwaites, R. and Freeston, M.H. (2005). Safety-seeking behaviours: Fact or function? How can we clinically differentiate between safety behaviours and adaptive coping strategies across anxiety disorders? *Behavioural and Cognitive Psychotherapy, 33*(2), 177–188. https://doi.org/10.1017/S1352465804001985

Westgate, E.C., Wormington, S.V., Oleson, K.C, and Lindgren, K.P. (2017). Productive procrastination: Academic procrastination style predicts academic and alcohol outcomes. *Journal of Applied Social Psychology, 47*(3), 124–135.

Wohl, M.J.A., Pychyl, T.A, and Bennett, S.H. (2010). I forgive myself, now I can study: How self-forgiveness for procrastinating can reduce future procrastination. *Personality and Individual Differences, 48*(7), 803–808. https://doi.org/10.1016/j.paid.2010.01.029

Zurita Ona, P. (Host). (2021, June 9). Dr. Z. on values (No. 23) [Audio podcast episode]. In *Playing-it-Safe Podcast*. https://www.thisisdoctorz.com/playing-it-safe-podcast

NOTES